ACROPOLIS
AND MUSEUM

TEXT AND PHOTOGRAPHS
BY SPYROS MELETZIS
AND HELEN PAPADAKIS

PUBLISHED BY SCHNELL & STEINER MUNICH & ZURICH
SOLE DISTRIBUTION IN GREECE: HELEN PAPADAKIS, ATHENS

Text and all photographs by Spyros Meletzis, Athens, and Helen Papadakis, Athens. The text was translated from Greek, into German by Antigone Papadakis, Athens, and revised by Ludwig Haberl, Munich. English translation by P. J. Dine, Munich. — Cover and graphic design by Nikos Perakis, Athens. The front cover shows a photograph of a kore (Museum No 670), the back cover a view from the Parthenon over Philopappos Hill to the Saronic Gulf and its islands.

BIBLIOGRAPHY

Homer, Iliad and Odyssey. — Pindar, Olympia vii. — Herodotus, History bks v, viii. — Thucydides, History of the Peloponnesian War i, ii. — Xenophon, Hellenica i. — Isocrates, Panathenaicus. — Plutarch, Themistocles, Pericles. — Pausanias, Description of Hellas: Attica.

Barthélemy A., Voyage du jeune Anacharsis en Grèce, 1839. — Bury J. B., A History of Greece, New York. — Cloché P., Le Siècle de Périclès, Paris 1949. — Coulanges Fustel de, La Cité Antique, Hachette. — Decharme P., Mythologie Grecque. — Dinsmoor W. B., American Journal of Archaeology vcl.LI, 1947. — Glotz G., La Civilisation Egéenne, Paris 1923. — Harrison Jane, Prolegomena to the study of Greek Religion, New York 1955. — Jardé A., La Formation du Peuple Grec, Paris 1923. — Lullies R. and Hirmer M., Greek Sculpture, London. — Miliadis J., Acropolis, Athens. — Orlandos A., Greek Architecture, Athens. — Payne H. and Mackworth-Young G., Archaic Marble Sculpture from the Acropolis, London. — Pettazoni R., La Religion dans la Grèce Antique, Paris 1953. — Picard Ch., La Sculpture Antique, Paris 1926. — Picard Ch., La Vie dans la Grèce Classique, Paris 1954. — Rangavi A., Dictionary of Greek Archaeology, Athens 1888. — Richepin J., Nouvelle Mythologie Illustrée, Paris. — Schrader H.-Langlotz E., Die Archaischen Marmorbildwerke der Akropolis, 1939. — Seyffert O., A Dictionary of Classical Antiquities, New York 1957. — The Large Greek Encyclopaedia, P. G. Makris Edition, Athens 1927. — Les Guides Bleus, Athènes, Hachette, 1960. — J. Miliadis, A Concise Guide to the Acropolis Museum, Athens 1965.

The drawing on page 3 has been prepared from a design by Prof. Gorham P. Stevens.

NINTH EDITION 1978   ISBN 3 7954 0554 8

SOLE DISTRIBUTOR FOR GREECE: HELEN PAPADAKIS, 15 PEFKON ST., ATHENS 625

THIS FORMS VOLUME 49/50 IN THE "GROSSE KUNSTFÜHRER" (ART GUIDES) SERIES OF OUR PUBLISHING HOUSE. EDITORS OF THE SERIES: DR. HUGO SCHNELL AND DR. PAUL MAI. EDITOR OF THE VOLUMES ON GREECE: DR. JOHANNES STEINER, MUNICH. — © 1967 BY VERLAG SCHNELL & STEINER GMBH & CO, MUNICH AND ZURICH. — PRINTED BY THE PUBLISHERS AT D-8595 WALDSASSEN / OPF.

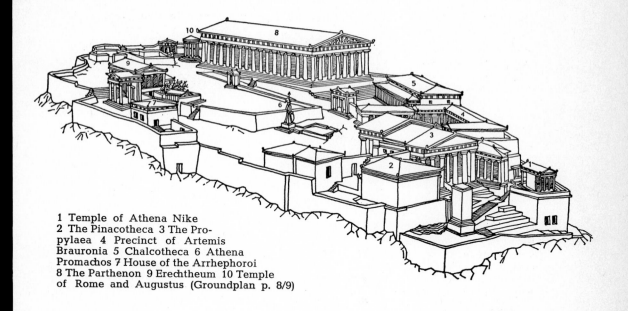

1 Temple of Athena Nike
2 The Pinacotheca 3 The Propylaea 4 Precinct of Artemis
Brauronia 5 Chalcotheca 6 Athena
Promachos 7 House of the Arrhephoroi
8 The Parthenon 9 Erechtheum 10 Temple
of Rome and Augustus (Groundplan p. 8/9)

THE ACROPOLIS

A rocky hill rises from the Attic plain, from the heart of the city of Athens; it is
the " Acropolis ", of all hill-top citadels surely the most famous. The extraordinary
attraction this hill exerts on men is to be accounted for by its harmonious beauty
and its wealth — still great in spite of past ravages — of monuments of inestimable
cultural value, but no less by the recollection that this hill was rendered sacred by
its choice as the privileged site of the temples and much venerated sanctuaries of
the gods, especially of Athene, divine protectress of the city, and, last but by no
means least, by the incomparable panoramic view of city, surrounding countryside
and sea which the visitor enjoys from its crown.
If we direct our gaze full circle, we catch the blue shimmer of the waters of the
Saronic Gulf to the south, and the distant glisten of mountains: Mt. Hymettus to
the east, Mt. Parnes to the north and, between these and to the west, Mt. Pentelicus
and Mt. Aegaleos.
These mountains are already familiar to us from the writings of early Attic authors.
But what the Attic masters of this early period produced in works of architecture
and plastic art, all this was subject to the transforming impact of time. Was all this
swept aside with the end of the era?
One thing is certain: when there is talk of the headsprings of European, indeed of
human culture in general, then that source which gushed forth in ancient Greece
must always be lauded as being among those that have never run dry. Athens
acted as the great catchment point which fed this stream most generously: as
centre of science and philosophy, queen of drama, and home of the fine arts.
The most venerable witness to the artistic creativeness of ancient Athens is its
proud citadel, the Acropolis.
Every day numerous visitors climb this sacred hill, with a greater or lesser sense

3

of expectation, in order to view at first hand the white marble monuments which crown it. These buildings — the Propylaea, the Temple of the Wingless Victory, the Erechtheum, the Parthenon — stand there as if struck from the very rock, but of their pristine glory little is now to be seen.

No gods adorn their pediments, no centaurs battle on their metopes, no joyful participants in the Panathenaic procession stride the temple frieze. The cella of the Parthenon no longer houses the gold and ivory statue of Athena Parthenos by Phidias, and we search the vestibule in vain for the Athena Promachos. These monuments meet our gaze today stripped of all adornment, the toll of time. Wherever we tread, fragments of marble litter our way. The destruction and devastation wrought by man have done even more than time to rob this artistic centre of its sublime beauty. Of the numberless statues which once filled the sacred precincts not one stands in its place today.

But the voice of the past still speaks to us even out of these temple ruins and tells us of the former splendour of these sacred buildings, which were not only renowned in their own day but can still rank as monuments to classical architecture and the creative power of man.

On our way to the Acropolis, the Temple of Nike Apteros or Wingless Victory catches our attention. Its slender and noble lines grace a steep ridge on the western side of the sacred hill and adorn, together with the Propylaea, the entrance to the Acropolis. The modern road follows the course of the Sacred Way. This, too, was paved, and along it the Panathenaic procession, with the numerous animals required for sacrifice, made its solemn progress. Arrived at the top, we pass the Propylaea with the Doric and the surviving halves of the Ionic columns of the interior. At times we walk on marble slabs, at others on bare rock. And so we arrive at last at the sacred enclosure of the Acropolis. What a splendour of marble greets us in the dazzling sunlight! The sanctuary of Athena Parthenos in all its Doric majesty! This temple, now bare and in ruins, almost entirely stripped of its wealth of plastic and painted interior adornment, still stands four-square on its foundations, defying the ravages of both time and weather. In spite of the vandalism it has been prey to in the course of some two and a half millenia, it is still today able to radiate something of its former splendour.

The Parthenon is one of those masterpieces which time has not been able to subdue. Men have plundered its treasures, but the Attic sun has lovingly kissed its white Pentelic marble and imparted to it a golden lustre. Its external appearance has changed in the course of the centuries, but its shell still rises in proud majesty and witnesses to the perfection and harmony of its lines, to the flawlessness of its Doric architecture. The beholder is astounded when he sees how the ancient Greeks were able to solve almost 2500 years ago problems of aesthetics and perspective which still puzzle experts today.

The Erechtheum, a graceful temple in the Ionic style, forms a contrast to the virile form of the Parthenon. This small sanctuary is situated to the left of the latter on the northern side of the Acropolis. On the side facing the Parthenon, six powerful maidens in long flowing Chitons bear on their heads the roof of the south-western porch of the temple.

The Erechtheum (Erechtheus = Earth Shaker is an ancient name for Poseidon) was venerated as more sacred than any other building on the Acropolis because, according to the legend, two great gods, Athene and Poseidon, once contended here for the possession of, and tutelary rights over, the city. Excavations have shown that the most ancient buildings of Mycenaean times also stood on this site.

The Acropolis (512 feet high) is not the only rock to rise out of the Attic plain.

4

There were others, too, like Mt. Anchesmus (Turcovuni), Mt. Lycabettus, which rises to a height of some 910 feet, and Museum Hill (today Philoppapos). But only the rock hill of the Acropolis, with an upper plateau 984 feet in length and 492 feet in width, with fresh water springs and caves at its foot, precipitous on three sides and accessible only from the west, offered the natural requirements for a citadel and for a settlement capable of defending itself.

Various indications serve to confirm the supposition that the Acropolis with the area surrounding it had been settled since the early Stone Age, but only the Mycenaean era particularly from c. 1400—c. 1200 B. C., brought a period of growth and prosperity. The Mycenaean Period

The Acropolis of Athens was built on the same model as the hill citadels at Mycenae and Tiryns. A wall constructed of large irregular blocks, some 15—20 feet thick and over 32 feet high, enclosed the hill top and reinforced the natural fortress. This cyclopean wall, the oldest construction on the Acropolis, was known as the Pelasgian wall, because the ancient Greeks believed it was built by the Pelasgians, who had inhabited Greece in pre-Hellenic times. According to Herodotus, the Pelasgians living in Athens were called " Cranians " and the Acropolis " Cranaa ". Access to the Acropolis was, at all periods, from the west, the only side which does not decline precipitously. To the right of the entrance, on the south-western side, on a ridge of the rock where today the Temple of Nike Apteros stands, the Pelasgians built a bastion, from which their soldiers could with greater safety pick off any foes from their side undefended by armour, if they ventured the ascent. The Pelasgians

In the 10th century B. C., the Pelasgian wall, which enclosed the rock was, although in itself complete, reinforced by an additional wall, which enclosed the Spring of Clepsydra, some sanctuaries, and especially the approach to the citadel. This wall had nine gates, hence its name Enneapylon.

The royal palace with its adjoining buildings and the dwellings of the nobles were situated within the walled enclosure. The houses of the common folk, however, stood outside the wall, at the foot of the hill and to the south, and only in times of danger did all seek refuge within the protective wall. The Royal Palace

The royal palace with its throne-room lay on the site today occupied by the Erechtheum. Sections of the foundations were uncovered at a depth of some 5 feet below the surface, but the excavations were afterwards filled in again. Today only the bases of two columns of porous stone are still to be seen, they are remains which date from the early historical period (near the Caryatids, behind an iron grill). The bases supported wooden columns which in turn bore the weight of the roof.

Not far from the palace, in the northern wall and somewhat to the east of the Erechtheum, there was a side exit for descent from the Acropolis. Sixteen steps hewn out of the solid rock are still to be seen.

According to Pausanias, Actaeus is said to have been the first king of Attica, which was at that time known as Actaea. On his death, Cecrops, his son-in-law, took over the government of the country. Cecrops lived during the early historical period, the socalled mythological or heroic period, and probably reigned from 1654 —1604 B. C. He was the founder of the city of Athens and its first king. The Acropolis, which until then had been called Cranaa, was renamed Cecropia and its inhabitants were known as the Cecropidae. In historical times many believed that Cecrops came from Egypt and had come to Attica as a settler. The Athenians, however, who gloried in being autochthonous and regarded Cecrops as a son of the earth, represented him symbolically as half man, half animal: he was human in his upper parts and a snake or dragon in his lower. The Prehistorical Period Cecrops

During the fifty years of his reign, Cecrops laid the bases of public morality. He

5

founded the supreme court (Areios pagos), enacted laws governing marriage and safeguarding private property, and taught men to bury their dead. Till Cecrops became king, the inhabitants of Attica lived in separate and independent family groups or clans; each clan had its own head, tutelary god, traditions, customs, and legends. Cecrops united them into the twelve independent Attic communities, each with its own tutelary god, altar and king, prytaneum and council chamber. All twelve demes were bound to the worship of Zeus Hypatos and Athena Polias on the Acropolis. He also set up altars to the gods Cronus and Rhea. Furthermore, Cecrops introduced new forms for religious service, and replaced the human, indeed all bloody, sacrifices to the gods with offerings of wheat and honey-cakes.

The Diipolia The Diipolia was a festival celebrated in Athens on the 14th of the month Sciro-phorion (mid June — early July) in honour of Zeus Polieus, the city's protector. This festival was also known as the " Bouphonia " because the " killing of an ox " was connected with it. The sacrificial ox was led to the Acropolis before the altar of Zeus, in front of which wheat and barley had been strewn. Hardly had the animal touched the nourishment consecrated to the god than a priest killed it by striking it on the head with an axe. Having done this, he cast the axe aside and fled. In his absence the axe was put on trial in the prytaneum, sentenced to death, and thrown into the sea. This unique rite shows that, although an ox was sacrificed during this festival, the shedding of blood before the altar was looked upon as blameworthy.

The Contest between Poseidon and Athene It is during Cecrop's reign that tradition placed the struggle between the two great gods, Poseidon and Athene, for the possession and protection of Attica. We are told that Poseidon, to show his might, struck the rock so forcibly with his trident that salt water immediately gushed forth, and that Athene lunged at the ground with her lance and immediately an olive tree sprang forth. The Olympian gods who were present with Cecrops at this contest as judges pronounced Athene the winner because she had made the Athenians a present of a plant till then unknown and of such usefulness to man. The spot where the gods left visible traces of their might was revered as the holiest on the Acropolis.

The Legend of Erichthonius Cecrops, whose son Erysichthon died young, had three daughters, Aglauros, Herse and Pandrosos. Tradition informs us of their fate. Gaea han consigned Erichtho-nius, her son by Hephaestus, to Athene for her to educate and raise. Athene enclosed him in a chest, giving this to the daughters of Cecrops with explicit instructions not to open it. The inquisitive sisters, Aglauros and Herse, did not keep the goddess's command and opened the chest. When they saw the child therein with a snake coiled round it, they were so frightened that, maddened with fear, they cast themselves down from the Acropolis to their deaths. Pandrosos became the first priestess of Athene. Her sanctuary, the Pandroseum, stood near the temple of the goddess in the west, where the silver-green olive tree eternally blossomed. In this temple Erichthonius grew to manhood.

After his death, the Athenians honoured Cecrops as a god and buried him in a tomb near the places hallowed by the gods.

After Cecrops, 17 kings occupied the throne of Athens over a period of 560 years.

Cranaus Amphictyon Cranaus, the strongest of the Athenians, was his successor, and the deluge which only Deucalion and Pyrrha survived was said to have taken place during his reign. Amphictyon, the son of Deucalion and husband of Cranaus' daughter, deposed his father-in-law and reigned in his stead, until he and his house with him were deprived of the throne by Erichthonius.

Erichthonius or Erechtheus Erichthonius or Erechtheus, king of Athens, enjoyed the very special protection of Athene (Homer: Iliad ii, 546—549). Born on the Acropolis, he was cared for and

6

raised by the goddess herself. The Athenians regarded him as their ancestral father. In his speech the " Panathenaicos ", Isocrates speaks with pride of the "divine
origin " of the Athenians and calls them " autochthonous ". He says that they
alone of all the Greeks were neither immigrants nor of mixed blood; on the contrary, they were descended from Erichthonius, who was born on the Acropolis of
Hephaestus and Gaea. He also maintained that the later kings of Athens down to
Theseus were all descended from this selfsame Erichthonius, who, like Cecrops,
was represented in art with a man's upper and a snake's lower body. Beneath the
shield of Phidias' chryselephantine Athena lay a coiled serpent, a symbol for Erechtheus. As faithful companion of the goddess he was represented as a serpent at
her feet.

Erechtheus established the worship of Athene. In the temple on the Acropolis
which he consecrated to her he placed the cult statue of Athena Polias, the tutelary
deity of the city. This statue was of olive wood. It was regarded as a gift from
heaven, and was thus highly revered. Erechtheus was also honoured in this temple
alongside Athene and Poseidon, and from this fact it has drawn its name, the
Erechtheum. The Cecropidae became known as Athenians and their city as Athens
for the first time under Erechtheus (Herodotus viii, Urania 44). Erechtheus also
founded the Panathenaea, which was at first known as the Athenaea. The invention
of the fourwheeled chariot is also attributed to him. As a reward for this invention,
Zeus allowed him to ride up into heaven and placed him among the constellations
as " Auriga " (the " Charioteer ").

Theseus was the most important of the many Athenian kings of mythological and   Theseus
early historical times. His father, Aegeus, was descended from Erechtheus; his
mother Aethra was a daughter of Pittheus of Troezen in the Peloponnese, who was
himself a son of Pelops, the most important king of the peninsula which was named
Peloponnesus after him. If in Antiquity Heracles (Hercules) enjoyed great honour
as a hero, indeed even as a god, throughout the whole of Greece, the special hero
of Athens was still Theseus. Inspired by the heroic deeds of Heracles, he took him
as his model and soon distinguished himself by his brave deeds in ridding the
country of robbers and wild animals which were devastating the land and plaguing
the inhabitants. The greatest of his heroic exploits, which brought him particular
renown, was the killing of the Minotaur in the Labyrinth of Crete.

Androgeus, son of Minos and Pasiphae, had travelled to Athens from Crete and
had taken part with extraordinary success in the contests organised in connection
with the Panathenaea, which had been founded shortly before. He was, however,
killed by the Bull of Marathon, which he chanced to meet. Whereupon Minos,
believing that the Athenians were to blame for his son's death, appeared before
Athens with his fleet, defeated the Athenians in battle, and demanded that they
send him, for a period of 9 years, an annual tribute of seven noble youths and seven
noble maidens, who were shut up in the Labyrinth of Crete to be devoured by the
Minotaur. When in the third year the fatal ship was about to set sail with the
youths and maidens selected by lot, Theseus was allowed, at his own earnest en-
treaty, to accompany the victims. Aegeus gave him white sails to take with him
which were to be hoisted instead of the black, if he were to return as victor. With
the help of Ariadne whose affections he had won, Theseus was able to vanquish
the Minotaur in the Labyrinth and by rewinding the magic thread find his way out
of the cave again safe and sound.

When now the ship was being made ready for the return journey, Theseus and his
companions forgot in their rejoicing to hoist the white sails. King Aegeus used to
look with longing from the Acropolis and keep watch for the ship which was to

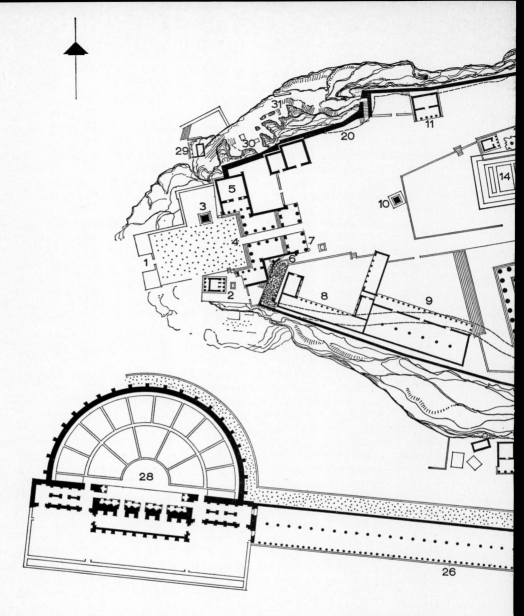

1 Beulé Gate 2 Temple of Athena Nike 3 Foundations of the Agrippa Monument 4 Propylaea 5 Pinacotheca 6 Remains of the Pisistratid Propylaeum and of the Pelasgian Wall 7 Sanctuary of Athena Hygeia (Health) 8 Temenos of Artemis Brauronia 9 Chalcotheke and Temenos of Athena Ergane 10 Athena Promachos 11 House of the Arrephoroi 12 Pandroseum 13 Erechtheum 14 Ancient Temple of Athena Polias 15 Altar of Athene 16 Parthenon 17 Temple of Rome and Augustus 18 Shrine of Zeus Polieus 19 Temple of the Hero Pandion 20 Pelasgian Wall 21 Odeum of Pericles 22 Old and New Temple of Dionysus Eleutherium 23 Theatre of Dionysus 24 Monument of Thrasyllus 25 Monument of Nicias 26 Stoa of Eumenes 27 Sanctuary of Asclepius 28 Odeum of Herodes Atticus 29 Clepsydra Spring 30 Cave of Pan 31 Ancient Stairway 32 Shrine of Eros and of Aphrodite " in the Gardens "

For this plan of the Acropolis we are indebted to the architect and archaeologist, John Travlos, Athens.

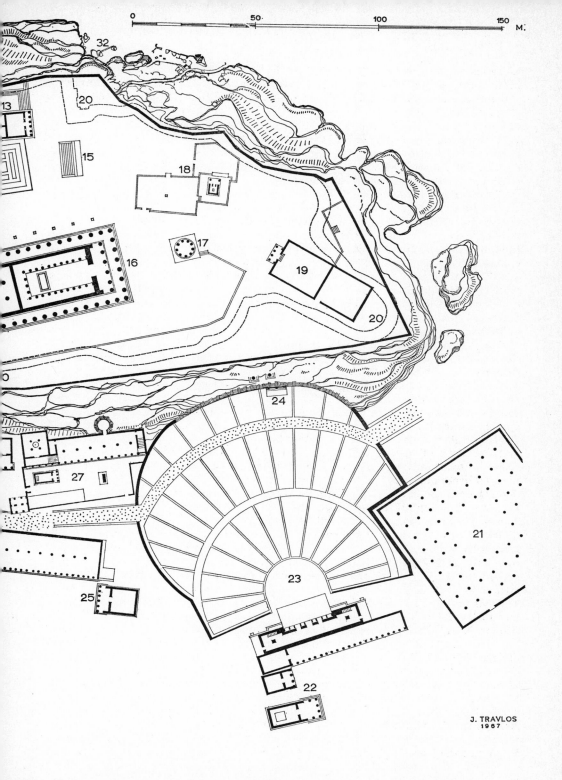

bring his son back to him. When he saw it making for the Bay of Phaleron with the black sails hoisted, he threw himself down from the rock in despair, thinking his son was dead. In ancient times his tomb was beneath the " pyrgos " of the Athena Nike.

The great political achievement of Theseus, now king of Athens, was to unite the 12 till-now-independent demes of the Attic and Megaran plains into one state with Athens as its centre. The links between the various cities of Attica had arisen much earlier. But Theseus, who maintained friendly relations with Crete, the most powerful and civilised state of his day, brought new ideas and forms into political and social life. For this reason tradition honours him as the founder of the Attic state.

Thucydides recounts (B. 15) how Theseus remodelled much, abolished the parliaments and administrative organs of the other cities and centred everything on Athens with one council chamber and one prytaneum (town hall). He allowed the inhabitants to cultivate their lands as previously, but compelled them to have one common city-state, Athens. In this way, Athens grew to be a great power, and as such Theseus handed the city on to his successors. The general assembly of parliament was divided into three classes: the nobles, the farmers and the artisans. The government of Athens already had democratic features at this date, but Theseus remained head of state and guardian of the law. A great festival called Synoikia or Metoekia, was founded to celebrate the union of the cities and ethnic groups of Attica. The Athenaea, the festival founded by Erechtheus in honour of Athena Polias, now took on greater significance and was renamed the " Panathenaea ", a splendid feast, in which all the united demes took part.

Just as Heracles had founded the Olympic Games in honour of Zeus and in memory of his heroic deeds, so Theseus founded the Isthmian Games in honour of Poseidon and his own great deeds. Thucydides says that " before Theseus the city enclosed only the Acropolis and the region at the foot of the southern slopes ". Theseus enlarged the city, erected state buildings like the prytaneum, parliament and the court of justice, and commissioned new homes to be erected for many aliens whom he invited to Athens to boost the population. They came from other parts in great numbers; so, too, did many nobles from the various cities of Attica. Soon the Acropolis was no longer able to accommodate so many inhabitants. Thus, a new city gradually came into being at the foot of the Acropolis towards the south-east along the banks of the Ilissus and near the Callirrhoe Spring. There the district " to asty " inhabited by the nobles or Eupatrids grew up. North of the Acropolis, tradesmen and artisans gradually settled. This accounts for the rise of the Ceramicus (Potters' Field), and other regions where the various professional groups settled. The Acropolis was simply called the " Polis "; only many centuries later did it become known as the " Acropolis ".

Theseus took part with other heroes of his day in the Expedition of the Argonauts and in the famous Calydonian Boar Hunt. He fought with Heracles against the Amazons and distinguished himself, at the side of his friend Pirithous, king of the Lapiths, in the battle against the Centaurs in Thessaly. These celebrated deeds of Theseus and the other heroes have provided many later artists with the inspiration for their themes in the decoration of monuments and other works of art.

Theseus' successor on the throne of Athens was Menestheus, son of Peteus, who led the Athenians against Troy in the Trojan War, during which he also met his death (1180 B. C.).

After this war, which had cost the Greeks great sacrifices in spite of their final victory, came the great event which threw the whole country into confusion: the coming of the Heraclidae and the Dorians, who migrated from northern Greece to the south around 1100—1000 B. C. These Dorians did not remain in Attica, but The Coming of the Dorians moved down to the Peloponnese, which they settled from end to end. Hordes of expelled Achaeans emigrated, many to Thracia, others to Crete and Asia Minor. Entire families of nobles, descendants of King Nestor of Pylos, took refuge in Athens. The Ionians, who inhabited the north-western region of the Peloponnese, Aegialea, were forced to abandon their 12 Ionian cities to the fleeing Achaeans and to seek new homes in Attica, which hospitably welcomed all expellees.

The Dorian Migration forms the great divide between two epochs of Greek history: between the Bronze Age and the Iron Age. The Dorians devastated much on their way and ushered in a period of cultural decline. Greece sank into a Dark Age which was to last for centuries.

The Dorians, who on their way south had not penetrated into Attica, now set out from the Peloponnese to punish the Athenians for giving hospitality to their enemies. Having conquered the province of Megara, they besought the Delphic Oracle to tell them which side would be victorious. They received the answer that that army would win whose leader fell.

When Codrus, who was king of the Athenians at the time and consumed with love Codrus 1044 B. C. for his country and people, heard this, he entered the enemy camp disguised as a peasant, provoked a quarrel there and was killed. Codrus' example moved the Athenians and filled them with such enthusiasm that they rushed into battle and forced the Dorians to retire.

After the death of Codrus (1044 B. C.), the Athenians abolished the kingship out of admiration for Codrus' spirit of sacrifice; they realised that Codrus had so ennobled his office that only a god would be worthy to wear the crown. Later rulers were therefore called " archons ". They were elected for life and had to answer to the people for their deeds. The first archon was Medon, the eldest son of Codrus. Two other sons, Neleus and Androclus, led the Ionians and as many of the Athenians who wanted to follow them to colonise the west coast of Asia Minor, The Ionian Colonies in Asia Minor because the population of Attica had grown so considerably. In Asia Minor the Ionians from the Peloponnese founded their twelve Ionian cities again, of which Miletus and Ephesus were destined to become the most important.

Two centuries after the Ionian colonisation, about 850 B. C., while Greece was Homer 850 B. C. The Iliad & the Odyssey gradually recovering from the terrible results of the Dorian migrations, an extraordinary figure illuminated the Greek world: Homer, the first in time among the great poets of all time. His immortal epics, the Iliad and the Odyssey, have become the pillars of Europe's culture and intellectual aspirations.

After 10 archons, chosen from Medon's line, had ruled over them, the Athenians The Archons began to limit the power and reduce the term of office of the archons, until finally, at the end of the 6th century, Cleisthenes, and later Aristides, expressly stipulated that nine archons were to be elected annually, each with his own particular duties. Eligible for the archonship were members of all property-classes.

With the death of Codrus the first chapter of the history of Athens came to a close, Mythology and History that of the mythological and heroic period.

The mythology of ancient Greece is so firmly intertwined with its history that it is nearly always difficult to extract the historical core from the myths and legends. The myths, which generally tell of improbable happenings depicted with fairy-tale charm, often conceal important doctrines or even historical truths, which can rarely be distinguished from the symbolism and fantasy of the mythological envelope. At a time when the art of writing was as yet unknown, the various data and happenings of early historical times were more easily handed down from generation to generation in the form of fairy tales or myths. Mythological tradition arose in this way.

Even historical events which reflect the fate of a whole people were at times attributed to individual mythical personages, e. g. an important chieftain or tribal leader. Thus the Deucalion myth makes an involved historical happening more intelligible to his descendants: it deals with the various Greek stems — the Achaeans, the Aeolians, the Dorians and the Ionians — and their repeated migrations

The Legends concerning the Greek Tribal Stems

within the confines of Greece. Hellen, the son of Deucalion and Pyrrha, ancestor of the Hellenes and king of Phthia in Thessaly, had three sons: Aeolus, forefather of the Aeolians, Doros, forefather of the Dorians, and Xuthus. Xuthus was driven out by his brothers and fled to Attica, where he married the daughter of Erechtheus and had two sons by her: Achaeus and Ion (Euripides: Ion). But soon he had to flee from Attica as well and migrated to the north-western region of the Peloponnese, Aegialea (later Achaea), where he settled with his family. Here then the descendants of Ion founded their twelve cities.

Megaron and Temple

In speaking of the myth of Poseidon and Athene, we have already seen how these two deities came to be honoured on the Acropolis: the archaeologists have uncovered ancient traces of this veneration at a considerable depth on the northern side of the Acropolis, where formerly the king's palace also stood. At that time the king was both priest and judge.

The Naos or Temple had its origins in the ancient palace. The central and most beautiful room, the very heart of the palace, the throne and reception-room, also seemed to men worthy to serve as a dwelling for their god. It was called the megaron. The plans of the first cultic buildings were based on the megarons of Mycenaean times. (NAOS from " naio " = I dwell). The temple was built as the god's dwelling. The god in question was first and foremost the god of the city, its guardian: " Zeus Polieus ", " Athena Polias ".

Once the deity had a dwelling, it was a short step for artists to give him a human form, too. His image was regarded as the focal point of the temple. The plastic art of Antiquity therefore developed hand in hand with these early cultic constructions. The first statues (xoana) were of crudely finished and carved wood and represented the divinities in human form. The best of them were ascribed either to the god Hephaestus or to the mythological figure of Daedalus, the first sculptor of Greece. Men looked upon these divine images with awe, cared for them like living beings, washed them and provided them with nourishment, attendance and service.

The Old Erechtheum

The wooden statue (xoanon) of Athena Polias, the most sacred of them all, was of olive-tree wood and was believed to be a gift from heaven. It was housed in the temple of Athena Polias, which was part of the temple of Erechtheus. Remains of this ancient temple have not yet come to light. (Perhaps archaeologists will one day unearth them beneath the foundations of the Erechtheum). In any case, we know from tradition that this ancient temple contained much that was of interest: the venerable relics of the contest between the two gods — the precious olive tree of Athene and the " sea of Erechtheus ", the salt spring of Poseidon — and further the temple of Athena Polias, the temple of Erechtheus-Poseidon, the sanctuary of Pandrosos, the tombs of Cecrops and Erechtheus, and the altar of the hero Butes. Butes was the son of Pandion and the grandson of Erechtheus, and took part with Heracles, Theseus and other heroes in the Argonautic Expedition. He was the goddess's first priest in the temple of Erechtheus and ancestor of the family of the Butadae, from whom all Athene's priests were drawn. This temple was generally known as the Erechtheum, but sometimes also as the temple of Athena Polias, since this was after all the most sacred part of the Erechtheum. The Persians burnt this earlier Erechtheum down in 480 B. C., as Herodotus tells us (viii, 54—55).

From the earliest, pre-Hellenic times to the days of Pericles and after, Athene was the favourite goddess of the Athenians. The numerous temples which were raised in her honour at all periods were intended to show the tutelary goddess how deep was men's gratitude to her. The Homeric Hymns represent Athene to us as the dearly beloved daughter of Zeus, who could deny her nothing. She sprang fully armed from the forehead of the Father of the gods, Zeus; lofty Olympus shook and the broad earth trembled when Athene, the " exalted spirit " " full of might and power to protect her people ", brandished her spear. Solemn oaths were sworn on her name together with those of Zeus and Apollo. These three gods thus seemed to embody the fullness of divine power. As goddess of heaven she, like Zeus, disposed of thunder and lightning, which sunder the clouds and bestow the life-giving rain. In very early times she was honoured as the goddess of agriculture; she is said to have taught men the cultivation of the earth and the use of the plough. The " Chalceia " was a festival at which the invention of the plough was celebrated with loud rejoicing and sacrifices.

As goddess of war, Athena Pallas was distinguished by power and courage, but she was by no means wild and harsh. She was full of magnanimity, the embodiment of understanding, reason and good sense. She was the goddess of invention, of art and culture. She it was, too, who taught women the arts of weaving and embroidery. In their festivals and thanksgiving, the Greeks had recourse to her not only as protectress of the city, but also as goddess of agriculture and clever inventiveness. At the close of winter, the " Procharisteria " was celebrated, a festi- val during which prayers were offered for a rich harvest the following autumn.

The various religious festivals which were still celebrated in classical times grew up in connection with the reverence paid to Athena Polias in her cult statue. These were: the Plynteria, the Callynteria, the Scirophoria, the Arrephoria and, finally, the Panathenaea.

In spring, the Plynteria and the Callynteria were celebrated from 19th to 25th of the month of Thargelion (May-June). During the Plynteria, the temple of Athene was thoroughly cleansed. The wooden image of the goddess was divested of its garments and covered with a peplus (veil). In the meantime, the garments were meticulously washed. The veiled image was then carried to the sea at Phaleron in solemn procession. There it was washed in a ceremony shrouded in mystery and then brought back to its temple. The day on which this ceremony was performed was considered unlucky, so that no work was done.

The Plynteria was followed by the Callynteria. During this festival, the image of the goddess was again clothed and attired in its cleansed garments. Both these festivals fell at that time of the year when the fruits and the wheat were ripening.

The Scirophoria was kept on the 12th of the month of Scirophorion (late June) in honour of Athena Sciras. A procession passed from the Acropolis to Sciron, a village on the Sacred Way. There the victims were sacrificed. A huge white umbrella (skiron) protected the priestess of Athena and the priests of Poseidon and Helius (the sun-god) from the rays of the sun. This umbrella was the symbol of the festival and gave rise to its name. During the Scirophoria men besought the gods to protect the crops from the great heat of summer.

During this same summer month, the festival of the Arrephoria also fell. This, too, was celebrated in honour of Athene, but now as goddess of the potent blessing of the nocturnal dew. Four young girls, aged 7 to 11, performed the duties of Arre-phoroi. They were chosen each year from the noble families of Athens for the service of the goddess. Two of them began, immediately after they had been chosen, to weave the „ peplus " (robe) for the cult image of the goddess. The other two each received from the priestess of Athene, on the night of the festival, a basket whose contents were mysterious and known to no one. The two young maidens took the baskets on their heads and passed by night through an underground passage to the sanctuary of " Aphrodite of the Gardens ", where they deposited them and received others, just as mysterious, in their stead, which they brought back to the priestess of Athene. With this, both their mission and their term of service was at an end.

Oschophoria The Oschophoria was a festival held at the time of the grape harvest in honour of Athene and Dionysus. The most important of all the festivals which the Athenians had celebrated for centuries past was the Panathenaea, but of this we shall have more to say later.

As we have already said, the Dorian migrations inaugurated a period of cultural decline which affected the whole of Greece. This decline was to be attributed first and foremost to the emigration en masse of the forces which had maintained and furthered the culture of the land till then.

The Middle Ages of Greece This long epoch, which lasted from the year 1000 to roughly 650 B. C., has been called the Middle Ages of Greece. We have no exact knowledge of what was altered and changed on the Acropolis during these centuries, since no traces of monuments or other works of art have, until now, come to light, with the exception of Geometric Period 8th & 7th Centuries numerous fragments of Geometric vases. Attic vases of this Geometric period of the 8th and 7th centuries were also found to the south of the Acropolis in the course of the excavations carried out from 1955 to 1960 (Acropolis Museum, Room V).

After the abolition of the monarchy, it was the archons who lived and worked in Athens, which began to grow rapidly around the Acropolis particularly from the north-western to the north-eastern side.

The royal palace, as also the entire area of the Acropolis, was dedicated to the gods. At the end of the Geometric Period, during the 7th century, but particularly at the beginning of the 6th, the first large temples were erected in Greece. The excavations on the Acropolis (1885—1890) brought to light finds of Archaic art, sculp- Archaic Sculptures in Poros tured work in " poros " (tufa) and marble. That in tufa consists, for the most part, of sections of pediments which adorned earlier temples and treasuries. In studying this poros sculpture, the archaeologists are faced with the problem that so far the foundations of temples or treasuries to which these fragments could belong have never been uncovered. At any rate, these works deserve our respect not only as the creations of men who were quite obviously past masters of their art, but also as witnesses to the epoch which they represent.

The oldest of this pedimental sculpture is a representation of the " Hydra " (Heracles killing the Hydra of the Lernaean Spring), which perhaps adorned a treasury of the 6th century B. C. (cf. plate 35). All that we know with certainty today is that Archaic Temple of Athena Polias 6th cent. B. C. in the 6th century B. C. a large Archaic temple stood on the Acropolis between the Parthenon and the Erechtheum. This was shown conclusively by the excavations of 1885, which laid bare the foundations. The archaeologists at first named this temple the " Hecatompedon ". Then it was called the Athena Polias, to whom alone it appeared to be dedicated. Today it is called, for the sake of clarity, the Dörpfeld temple, after the German archaeologist who first made a thorough study of it. In any case we are presented with a problem: whereas the external foundations, which carried the " peristasis " (peristyle) are carefully constructed of great reddish-coloured blocks from the quarry at Karra, the internal seem to have been laid with less care. Without any real order, they are built of small chunks of blue limestone hewn from the Acropolis hill itself. These internal foundations were roughly 100 foot long (hence the name " Hecatompedon "). These facts led Dörpfeld and many other archaeologists to posit the hypothesis that this temple was built in two stages. According to this theory, the internal foundations are thought to have belonged to a temple which was built of tifa in the Doric style about the year 570 B. C. during the reign of Solon. It was an amphiprostylus with pedimental sculpture in poros. In contrast, the external foundations were to carry the colonnade, which was added much later (c. 525 B. C.) at the time of the Pisistratidae. This addition clad the temple in new splendour and magnificence.

Many years later, W. B. Dinsmoor made a thorough examination of this temple and all the finds which according to Dörpfeld and other archaeologists belonged to it (metopes, poros pedimental sculpture, architraves and so on). He maintained that his predecessors were mistaken and that all the foundations belonged to the Pisistratid temple of Athena Polias (American Journal of Archaeology 1947, vol. 51, pp. 109—151). Dinsmoor believed that a much older temple must have stood on the site of the Mycenaean palace. This temple was built after the destruction of the palace and survived until the closing years of the " tyranny " of Pisistratus (529), when it was pulled down. Of this temple nothing has remained. This " Geometric " temple must have been the " venerable old temple " which is mentioned in the texts. Parallel to this temple, a new one was raised in honour of the same goddess The Hecatompedon or Original Parthenon Athene in the southern region of the Acropolis. Its foundations have not been found, however, probably because they lie under the Parthenon. But the pedimental sculptures in poros, which are all of the same material, size, style and wealth of colour, and were all found on the same site, namely in the embankments of the great terrace to the south of the Parthenon, can only have formed part of the same pedimental decoration of one and the same temple.

After an exact examination of these architectural and sculptural finds, Dinsmoor attempts a reconstruction of this hypothetical temple, the real " Hecatompedon ", the original Parthenon, or, as Dinsmoor calls it, the " grandfather " of the present Parthenon.

According to his computations, this temple must have been 100 Doric feet in length (a little more than 107 English feet) and 50 Doric feet in width, i. e. a proportion of 1 : 2, which is a very probable proportion for a temple of the period in question. This " amphiprostylus " in the Doric style had 3 Doric columns at front and rear, a Doric frieze with 8 metopes and 9 triglyphs on the front facade, and 18 metopes and 19 triglyphs along both sides. Its height was 21 Doric feet. Its pediments were decorated with polychrome poros sculptures. The group with the lioness devouring a small bull is to be placed at the centre of the western pediment. A part of this group has survived — cf. plate 41, Acropolis Museum, Room I, No 4 —; to both sides, the two serpentine monsters (Room II, Nos 37—40) are to be located. The eastern front was adorned, according to Dinsmoor, with work of important sculptors; in the middle was the bull being killed by two lions (cf. plate 42, Room III, No 3), on both sides were other groups (cf. plate 36, Room II, No 35).

On the left-hand side of the tympanon, the struggle of Heracles with Triton, whose fish-tail fits into the angle, was depicted. On the right was a peculiar monster, the demon with three human bodies which merge below the trunk into three intertwined dragon-tails.

This temple must have been built in c. 570 B. C. and dedicated in 566.

About 561 B. C., Pisistratus, a noble from Brauron in Attica, seized power in Athens "Tyranny" of Pisistratus and the Pisistratidae 561-510 B. C. and had himself proclaimed tyrant on the Acropolis. The word tyrant did not, of course, have the meaning then that it has acquired in the course of time, that of a cruel and oppressive despot; it meant nothing more than unconstitutional sovereign, dictator. Pisistratus had three sons: Hippias, Hipparchus, and Thessalus. When he died in 528 B. C., Hippias succeeded him. The " tyranny " of Pisistratus and the Pisistratidae lasted roughly half a century and enriched Athens and the Acropolis with many magnificent monuments.

Propylaeum They embellished the entrance to the Acropolis with a propylaeum, a covered vestibule (55 feet 9 inches long and 44 feet 4 inches wide). This construction had four columns at the western end and four at the eastern, and was intended to protect the wooden doors at its centre from both sun and rain. Having passed through this propylaeum, one stood facing the temple of Athena Polias, which lay directly opposite. In the presentday Propylaea, an anta and 3 steps with a part of the Pelasgian wall are to be seen at the inside, south-eastern corner (cf. photograph, plate 14).

Return of Ionian Artists To the south-east of this propylaeum, Pisistratus commissioned a monumental altar to be raised in honour of the goddess Artemis, whose cult he had brought with him from his home town of Brauron. The Pisistratids advanced the arts and the sciences, and promoted trade and the navy. Their hospitality led them to open the doors of Athens to the nobles, poets, and artists of the Ionian cities of Asia Minor which had shortly before been taken by the Persians. These Greeks preferred to leave their cities and return to the land from which their forefathers had come 450 years before. Their return to Attica was to have a lasting effect on the intellectual and social life of the Athenians, and on the development of the fine arts. Masters of the art of sculpture in marble and of plastic work in bronze, after the fashion of Rhoecus of Samos and Theodorus, had an important influence on the workshops of Attica and left their mark on most of the artistic production of this period.

Temple of Athena Polias 525 B. C. The opponents of the Pisistratidae, the Alcmaeonidae had been banished to Delphi. There they had begun in the meantime to rebuild the temple of Apollo which had been consumed by fire. This they did more splendidly and beautifully, with magnificent marble sculptures on the pediments.

In their desire to outdo the Alcmaeonidae, the Pisistratidae wanted to endow Athena Polias with a new and sumptuous temple. They pulled down the " Geometric " temple, which, as we have already said, stood on the site of the Mycenaean palace, and built a new and imposing temple where, between the Parthenon and the Erechtheum, the excavated foundations are to be seen today.

The War of the Gods and the Giants This Archaic temple of Athena Polias was built in the Doric style, of tufa, and as a peripteros, i. e. surrounded by a single range of columns. It had six columns at the small ends, and 12 on the flanks. Of the pediments of this poros temple so far only four marble figures have been excavated: an Athene and three Giants. Taking these as their starting-point, the archaeologists attempt a reconstruction of the eastern pediment group. In all probability, the assault of the Giants on the Olympian gods was there depicted. But naturally there are gaps in the reconstruction. These statues of Parian marble (Acropolis Museum, Room V) date from the year 525 B. C.: the Athene, over 6 feet tall, dressed in a long " chiton " and " himation ", evidently stood in the centre with Zeus. In her right hand, which is missing, she must have been holding her spear and thrusting at one of the giants, on whom her gaze is fixed. With her left arm she spreads the " aegis " decorated with a fringe of snakes and the head of the Medusa to shield her body and to strike fear into her opponents. The two other giants fit into the corners of the pediment.

The interior of the temple was divided into two by a transverse wall. In the eastern section was the " sekos " or cella, the sanctuary which was divided into a nave and two aisles by two rows of three columns. In the centre against the wall, stood the cult statue of Athena Polias. The western part formed the " opisthodomos ", a large vestibule with two smaller rooms at the rear. Here, carefully arranged, stood the offerings made to the goddess. In one of these small rooms was stored the carefully guarded temple treasure. The interior of the temple, as also the courtyard

16

outside, was adorned with many Archaic statues of female figures, dedicatory statues to Athene.

These "kores" came to light quite unexpectedly near the Erechtheum and the northern wall during the excavations of 1886. Today they adorn the rooms of the Acropolis Museum.

These Archaic kores represent the art of the period from c. 550 to 490 B. C. and clearly reveal the extent of the Ionian influence on the art of this time. From the Doric Peplus Bearer No 679 (cf. plate 58, 59, and 120), which is dated c. 530 B. C., to the Euthydicus kore No 686 (cf. plates 87, 119), 490 B. C., we notice that all these kores, with the one exception of the first-mentioned, are wearing Ionian or Ionian-influenced clothing. Dorian dress differed considerably from the Ionian. Dorian attire is symmetrical and strictly proportionate; its lines are vertical and horizontal, and the resulting outline is clearcut. In contrast, Ionian dress employs oblique lines and is distinctly asymmetrical; the outline, too, is irregular. The Dorian peplus, which the women of Attica wore over a light shirtlike garment known as the chiton, was of wool; it hung straight down, with few folds below the girdle. The Ionian chiton, on the other hand, was the main article of attire. The outer garment thrown over it for outdoor wear was the himation. This was a type of shawl or rectangular cloth, of some soft, generally woollen, material. Two of the ends were fastened over the right shoulder with a clasp; the left shoulder was left uncovered. From the gathering at the right shoulder, it fell vertically in numerous folds, which are the special characteristic of the Ionian himation. Each woman could express her own personal taste and charm by the way she draped her himation. The Ionian artist excelled particularly in the vivid presentation of feminine grace and charm in sculpture. These kore figures raise the chiton slightly with their left hand, which thus throws the female form into delicate relief in a most attractive manner. The interplay of folds merges into an harmonious whole. In their right hand, the kores generally hold an offering.

Their coiffures are stylised archaically. Their variety and delicate grace could provide many a present-day hairdresser with his inspiration. The hair is tastefully swept up in waves adorning the forehead and hangs in graceful curls or tresses before the breast and down the nape of the neck. The hair, the eyes, and the lips of the kores were painted and traces of this paint can still be seen on some of them. Wax was rubbed into the faces to give them a yellowish tint. The hem of the chiton and the himation often reproduce colourful embroidery. The purely Ionian kores have somewhat slanting eyes and the "Archaic" smile on their lips.

This smile, which on the first Archaic kores is almost stereotyped, began to disappear towards the end of the 6th century. It was replaced by a serious expression which is characteristic of Attic art. After this latter had freed itself from the Ionian influence (500 B. C.), e. g. kore No. 684, kore No. 674. Kore No. 686, the "Pouting Maiden", a dedicatory offering of a certain Euthydicus, is the last of the surviving kores which has preserved the external characteristics of Archaic art, altough its visual expression inclines more to the spirit of the art of the pre-classical period, to the severe style.

All of these smiling kores, in spite of the many elements they have in common, show an unmistakable individuality. They were not portraits of ladies of the time, but statues dedicated to the goddess whose eyes were to be gladdened by their view. Thus, adorning the open space on the Acropolis in noble array, they lent, with their smiling grace and human candour, a hint of divine gaiety to the festivals celebrated in honour of Athena Polias.

The Panathenaea was the festival which excelled all others and was celebrated annually with great pomp and circumstance, not only by the Athenians, but by all the inhabitants of Attica. It was the oldest of the festivals, having been founded by Erechtheus in honour of Athena Polias. In the beginning it was of a purely religious and local character, for the Athenians presented the goddess, on the occasion of her birthday every year, with a peplus (veil): an ancient custom which Homer also mentions (Iliad vi, 297). Later, when Theseus united all the Attic demes with Athens as capital, the festival was transformed into a folk-festival, which from now on was called Panathenaea in stead of Athenaea. Pisistratus and the Pisistratids bestowed still greater importance and splendour on the Panathenaeic festival. They introduced the distinction between the lesser and the great festivals. The Lesser Panathenaea was celebrated annually, the Great only every four years, that is in the third year of the Olympiad from 24—29 Hecatombaeon (July/August). From the aristocratic festival of its origins it developed into a folk-festival, and from pan-Athenian it gradually became pan-Hellenic.

The Great Panathenaea consisted of two parts. During the first days of the festival, contests were organised which were at first mainly of an equestrian character. The last days were set aside for the religious celebrations, which were held on a splendid and large scale and formed the most sightworthy part of the celebrations. The equestrian contests consisted of horse- and chariot-races, and various acrobatic displays by the " apobatae ". The competitors came exclusively from the ranks of the rich. Pisistratus introduced athletic competitions as well in which the less well-to-do could take part. These comprised five types of contest: foot-races, wrestling, boxing, long jump and discus, and were arranged according to age-group: boys, youth, men.

The musical competitions occupied an important place in the celebrations. Pisistratus, who had established a learned body to collate and set in order a definitive text of Homer's works, now donated, among other things, prizes for rhapsodists who recited poems, especially excerpts from the Homerian epics, with effect.

At the Great Panathenaea, there were, besides the three main contests we have already mentioned (equestrian, athletic, and musical-poetical), some others of less importance, like the " Pyrrhic ", the " Euandria ", and the " Lampadedromy " or torchrace. The " Pyrrhic " was a war dance performed by men armed with shields and lances who mimed all the movements and phases of a real battle (cf. plate 113). According to tradition Athene was the first to perform this dance, in celebration of the victory of the gods over the Giants. The Athenians, who so admired powerful, virile beauty, organised a further contest called the " Euandria ", for which competitors were likewise divided into three groups.

The victors in the athletic games received as their prize a splendid amphora filled with oil, known as a " Panathenaic amphora ". This showed, on the one side, a representation of Athena Polias standing with shield and lance, with the inscription on the left side: Τῶν ᾿Αϑήνηϑεν ῎Αϑλων, and, on the other, a scene from the contest itself. The winner of the musical competitions was awarded a sum of money and a garland, while the victors of the " Pyrrhic " and the " Euandria " were presented with an ox as their prize.

The games were under the superintendence of ten " Athlothetae ", one drawn from each of the phylae or tribes. These officials were elected by the people for four years. The contests concluded with a phantasmagoric torch-race from the altar of Prometheus near the Academy to the centre of the city.

The last day of the festival, the 28th Hecatombaeon, the birthday of Athena Polias, was dedicated to the clothing of the cultic image of the goddess in the new peplus and to the solemn hecatomb. The peplus was of fine, yellow wool, which the " arrephoroi ", two little girls (cf. supra), and a host of " ergastinae ", older maidens chosen from the first aristocratic families, had painstakingly and artistically woven. This work was supervised by the priestess of Athene.

The peplus bore a gold-embroidered representation of the struggle between Athene and the Giants.

In a magnificent procession, prepared for with great pains and a delight for the pious onlooker, the peplus was conveyed from the Ceramicus to the Acropolis. In later times the peplus fluttered like a sail from the mast of a galley, which, moving on hidden wheels, appeared to be gliding along on its way. It took the position of honour at the centre of the procession.

The festal procession formed up on the open space of the Outer Ceramicus. At sunrise it moved off and passed through the Dipylon Gate and across the Inner Ceramicus to the Agora. It was headed by the priests, the archons, the magistrates and the strategi. There followed attendants leading the sacrificial animals (cf. plate 103, 109), then the " Canephoroi ", young Athenian maidens drawn from the leading families of the city and selected for their beauty, who " bore " on their heads light " baskets " containing presents for the goddess and the implements of sacrifice. Behind them came the " Skiadiphoroi " and the " Diphrophoroi ", young daughters of the " metoekoi " (immigrants), who carried " skiadia " (umbrellas) to shade the Canephoroi from the heat of the sun and " diphroi " (stools) for them to sit on. Representatives of the immigrants, the " Scaphephoroi ", brought trays with various offerings for the goddess. The " Hydriaphoroi " carried pitchers of water and honey for the sacrificial libations (cf. plate 106). Musicians with harps and flutes played and sang hymns in honour of the goddess. The " Thallophoroi ", venerable old men from all the Attic tribes, bore olive branches. Soldiers in full armour, charioteers and the famous, colourfully clothed Athenian cavalry formed the gorgeous conclusion of the procession.

The procession crossed the Agora, passed the Eleusinium, and then came to a halt in front of the Areopagus on its way up to the Acropolis. There the ship carrying the peplus, the cavalry and the chariots remained. The " ergastinae " took the peplus down from the mast, carried it up to the Acropolis and there delivered it to the priestess of Athene, who was waiting for them at the entrance to the temple.

After the presentation of the peplus, the victims were sacrificed on the great altar of Athena Polias and on the altars of Athena Nike and Athena Hygieia (health). Afterwards the flesh of the sacrificial animals was distributed among the people. The festive repast in the open air which followed lasted until the early hours of the morning.

During the Great Panathenaea held in the year 514 B. C., two young Athenians, Harmodius and Aristogiton, succeeded in assassinating Hipparchus, the younger son of Pisistratus, in the Ceramicus while the procession was still lining up. Harmodius was despatched on the spot by the Tyrant's bodyguard: Aristogiton died under terrible torture. Four years later, Hippias was also forced to leave his homeland Attica and go into exile in Persia. This marked the end of the " tyranny " of the Pisistratidae, which had lasted some 50 years. The long years of Pisistratid rule were, in spite of all Pisistratus had done for Athens, so hateful to the Athenians that they felt the tyrannicides should receive due honour for their deed. After all they owed them their liberty! Antenor, the great sculptor, was commissioned to execute a marble statue of the " Tyrannicides " to be raised on the Agora. (Kore No 681, cf. plate 93, and the pediment of the Alcmaeonid temple of Apollo in the museum at Delphi — cf. our guide to Delphi, p. 65 — are ascribed to this same artist.) The Persians later carried this statue off with them to their own

Harmodius
and
Aristogiton
514 B. C.

Antenor

19

land (c. 480 B. C.). After the victory won at the Battle of Salamis, the Athenians commissioned Critius and Nesiotes to execute a new bronze group of the " Tyrannicides ". (Statue No 698 in the Acropolis Museum, cf. plate 94, is also ascribed to Critius; it has been dubbed the " Critius Boy ".)

In the year 508/7 B. C. Cleisthenes, an Alcmaeonid, was able to induce the Athenians to support his sweeping reform of the constitution in a democratic spirit. But already the great threat to their existence was approaching from abroad.

By 500 B. C., King Darius of Persia had subjugated all the Greek cities of Asia Minor. In the struggle for their freedom only Athens had come to their aid. Now he intended first to " punish " Athens and then to subjugate the whole of Greece. In 490, a Persian fleet landed at Marathon.

Under Miltiades as general, the Athenians defeated the Persians in the Battle of Marathon and returned to Athens loaded with booty. This meant that the first Persian assault had been beaten off and Darius was forced to retreat.

During the years following, the Athenians desired to erect a new and splendid temple on the southern part of the Acropolis out of gratitude to their tutelary goddess. They therefore demolished the old " Hecatompedon " (according to Dinsmoor, p. 15), that is the original Parthenon, and laid the foundations for a new temple. The actual foundations were to be laid on a strong base of tufa. Since the ground slopes off abruptly towards the south and a difference in level of more than 35 ft had to be compensated for, a massive substructure had to be built. A little more than 62 ft further south, a solid retaining wall was built near the Pelasgian wall and the intervening space filled with rubble. As venerable remains, the pedimental poros sculpture of the Hecatompedon, together with a variety of other architectural sculpture, metopes, triglyphs and capitals, were buried in the rubble. The foundations of the temple were then laid on this substructure. The temple was to be 220 ft long and a little more than 77 ft wide. It was planned as a peripteros with six columns along front and back, and sixteen along both flanks. Hardly had they begun to erect the marble columns, however, when the Persians launched a large-scale attack on Greece's liberty. There followed the barbaric destruction of the Acropolis. This incomplete marble temple is known today as the " Older Parthenon " or, as Dinsmoor puts it, the " father of the Parthenon ".

Ten years after the Battle of Marathon, the Persians under King Xerxes fitted out a new expedition against Greece. This time they came with a large fleet and a mighty army levied from the multitude of peoples within the unwiedly Persian empire. They crossed the Hellespont and conquered the cities of northern Greece, which offered no resistance. The Persians eventually arrived at the narrow pass of
Thermopylae. Here the Greeks hoped to hinder the further progress of the Persian army. After the Greek position had been betrayed, the Persians threatened to encircle the Greeks. King Leonidas with his 300 Spartans, however, held off the Persians, enabling the largest part of the Greek army to retreat. Their heroic death was not to be in vain.

After Thermopylae, the Persians conquered Boeotia and advanced on Athens. After the sea battle at Artemisium (Euboaea), the Persian fleet sailed in line with the land forces to the Bay of Phaleron. Themistocles, who was the leading man in Athens at the time and had long before prevailed upon the Athenians to build up a large fleet, believed that victory was only to be gained at sea. Since he was unable to convince his fellow citizens (Plutarch: Themistocles x), he tried to influence them with divine signs and prophecies. The Athenians, for instance, believed that a monstrous snake, a symbole for Erechthonius lived in the Erechtheum and watched over the Acropolis (Herodotus viii, 41). Every month they

20

brought it offerings of honey cake, which were always consumed. On this occasion, however, they were found untouched. The priestess declared that the goddess had deserted the Acropolis to lead the Athenians to the sea. As for the Delphic oracle about the " wooden wall " behind which the Athenians should seek refuge, Themistocles interpreted this as meaning wooden ships and not the wooden wall around the Acropolis. The ships offered their only hope of salvation. In this way, Themistocles was able to convince the Athenians. They left the city; the old people, the women and children were brought to safety in Salamis and Troezen. All able men, on the other hand, went on board, accompanied by the venerable image of the goddess Athene. There they prepared for the great battle with the Persian fleet. When the Persians arrived at Athens, they found a city deserted of its inhabitants. They attempted to take the Acropolis but met with resistance. Some old people, the sanctuary guards and a good number of the poorer classes had sought refuge there. They had interpreted the oracle in their own way and had blocked the entrance to the Acropolis with door-leaves, window shutters, and planks of wood. They thought this put them out of harm's way.

The Persians began the siege from the Areopagus. They constructed fire-arrows with tow, ignited them, and hurled them up at the " wooden wall ". Altough this eventually burnt down, the besieged still held out. They rolled great stones down the slope and rejected all demands to surrender. The siege lasted several days. When a Persian force, however, managed to climb the northern slopes of the Acropolis unobserved and suddenly appeared before the defenders, these were so startled and overcome with fear that they either sprang over the precipice to their deaths or rushed into the Temple to seek the help of the goddess. The Persians forced the temple door, dragged the supplicants out and put them to death. They then proceeded to plunder and demolish the temples. With torches they set everything in flames. After this work of destruction, Herodotus tells us that Xerxes sent for the exiled Greeks in his retinue and bade them mount the Acropolis and offer sacrifices to their goddess there. They obeyed and entered the sacred precincts. Great was their surprise when they saw a new, foot-long sprouting from the burnt stump of the sacred olive tree (Herodotus viii, 52—55)!

Of all the battles which the Greeks fought against the Persians, the naval engagement at Salamis was the one which once for all rid Greece of the Persian threat, firmly established democracy in Athens, and won renown for all Greeks, especially for the Athenians. This success must be attributed, first and foremost, to the strategic plan evolved by Themistocles. When Xerxes saw the complete annihilation of his fleet, he hurried back to his own land, full of despondency and consternation. He left a sizable army behind, unter the command of Mardonius, which was to subjugate Greece. After eight months spent in Thessaly, Mardonius marched to Boeotia and from there sent an emissary to the Athenians to induce them to enter on a special agreement with the Persians. However, the Athenians replied: " For as long as the sun maintains its course, the Athenians will remain the sworn enemies of the barbarians, and they will never forgive them for the profanation of their gods and the desecration of their holy places." On receiving this answer, Mardonius marched against Athens, and occupied the city, which had again been deserted by its inhabitants, who had moved to Salamis. After having ravaged the city and demolished the walls and the sanctuaries, he returned to Boeotia.

The last land battle between Greeks and Persians, at which the latter sustained their heaviest losses, was fought at Plataea. Of 350,000 Persians only some 40,000

21

are said to have escaped with their lives. Mardonius, too, was among the fallen. This marked the end of the Persian wars of aggression.

After the withdrawal of the Persians, Themistocles advised his fellow citizens to fortify Athens with walls before getting down to the task of reconstructing their houses. The entire population collaborated in the work. The wall rose rapidly, because the workmen employed all and any material within reach. It seemed unimportant whether the stones were well dressed or not. They took columns from the ravaged temples, marble debris from the cemeteries, cornerstones from the ruined houses, and whatever else appeared suitable. All-important was that the work should be concluded rapidly. Themistocles then began to fortify Piraeus, for he recognised the importance of the fleet and of maritime trade for Athens.

On the Acropolis the temples were gutted and in ruins. The statues of the gods encumbered the ground and Athene, their protectress, had no roof over her head. First they tackled the work of removing all traces of the devastation. And since the Pelasgian wall had suffered damage in several places along the northern side, they fortified the Acropolis on its northern and north-western sides with a new wall, over 16 ft high and 13 ft wide. Much of the poros debris from the temple of Athena Polias was built into this wall: column drums, triglyphs, and metopes, among which were 12 unfluted marble drums from the " Old Parthenon ", which the Persians had destroyed. It is said that Themistocles ordered these relics to be so built into the wall that they could be seen by all and act as a perpetual reminder to the Athenians of the destruction wrought by the Persians. (This curious wall of Themistocles is still to be seen today on the northern side of the Acropolis.)

The Athenians carefully buried the shattered statues, kores and other sculptures dedicated to Athene, together with various relief fragments and inscriptions held in pious honour. They covered them with rubble to level the area behind the Themistoclean wall and in front of the north-eastern side of the Erechtheum. Although the ancient Greek texts give no certain information here, many archaeologists believe that the Athenians placed the venerable wooden statue of Athena Polias in the " opisthodomus ", the western section of the Pisistratid temple of Athena Polias, after hurriedly renovating it to this end; the temple treasure was also kept here. Dinsmoor and others, however, think this wooden image of the goddess was accommodated in a small roofed sanctuary located roughly on the site occupied by the eastern part of the later Erechtheum.

Cimon, the son of Miltiades, continued the work of Themistocles. He built a new wall on the southern and eastern sides of the Acropolis in 468 B. C. from the proceeds raised from the plunder he had collected after his brilliant victory over the Persians at the mouth of the Eurymedon. This wall, known as " Cimon's Wall ", did not run parallel to the Pelasgian wall along the edge of the rock but extended farther south. Now it was nearly 60 ft high and some 24 ft thick at the base and almost 18 ft thick at the top. This slanting of its external surface rendered this retaining wall still stronger so that it could without danger support the weight of the rubble which would enable the terrace to be extended and levelled.

During the days of Cimon, the Greeks had for their part launched an attack on the Persian empire, after liberating all the islands in the Aegean Sea and all the cities of Greece and Asia Minor. About the year 478/77, Aristides " the Just " invited representatives of the islands and the cities to Delos and there founded the first
Delian Confederacy. The Athenians were entrusted with the supreme command at sea and guaranteed to defend their allies against pirates and the Persians. The confederates paid tribute and supplied ships. The money which was contributed towards the league was stored at Delos. The administrative side of the Confederacy

devolved on the Athenians. Cimon was later sent to put down the revolt, when the islands of Thasos, which controlled the gold-mines on the Thracian coast, and of Naxos refused to pay their tribute to the Confederacy. He occupied Naxos, razed its fortifications, and imposed a fine on its citizens (469). He took the gold-mines away from the island of Thasus. These gold-mines and the silver-mines of Laurion (Attica), the booty won during the Persian wars and the treasure of the Delian Confederacy, which was later transferred from Delos to Athens, formed the financial basis upon which Pericles later relied when he commissioned the construction of the immortal monuments associated with his name on the Acropolis.

Cimon beautified the city of Athens and enriched it in many ways. He erected statues, planted trees and built stoas or colonnades, he commissioned Polygnotus, the painter, and the latter's friends, Micon and Panaenus, the brother of Phidias, to adorn the " Stoa Poikile " or Painted Colonnade with frescoes. From the year 478 onwards, Athens bore the main brunt of the wars of liberation against the Persians. Attica had been hit hard; its reconstruction made heavy demands on its population. The fighting lasted, with short interludes, until about 450 B. C. An expedition was even sent to the land of the Pharaohs. Such times were not favourable to the allocation of comprehensive and costly public contracts to architects and artists. In contrast, in Aegina and the Peloponnese, where the cities were not visited by the vandalism of the barbarians, artists were able to raise magnificent temples to the honour of their gods and the glory of their fatherland.

Shortly after the naval battle of Salamis (480), the Aeginetans raised a grand pe- ripteral temple in the Doric style to their goddess Athena Aphaea. The pediments were decorated with magnificent sculptures in marble. A similar temple was also built at Olympia in Zeus' honour with sculptures in marble vigorously depicting mythological subjects, many other works of art in marble and bronze.

At this time a great host of artists are said to have glittered on the firmament of Greek art. But their works, indeed even the names of many of them, are lost in oblivion. Among the most famous of those whose names have come down to us, the following were particularly outstanding: Onatas of Aegina, Canachus of Sicyon, and Ageladas of Argos, who enjoyed a wide reputation as exponents of the fine arts. The last named distinguished himself particularly in being the teacher of the three greatest sculptors of the Classical period: Myron from Attica, Phidias of Athens, and Polyclitus of Argos.

About the year 470, the sculptor Calamis was active at Athens. The ancient docu- ments inform us that the works of Calamis in marble and bronze represented the culmination of the " severe style ". Calamis was Cimon's artistic adviser, just as Phidias was later Pericles'. Whereas the temple of Athena Aphaea at Aegina and of Zeus at Olympia stood in proud splendour, the Acropolis rock remained almost naked of temples and monuments for nearly thirty long years (480—447 B. C.). It was the state whose pious obligation it was to make good the damage which the barbarians had done to the temples of the gods and thus show the town's tutelary goddess the people's gratitude for her gracious favour. After all she had helped them to win the battles of Marathon and Salamis; she had not suffered them to become the slaves of the barbarians; with her help they had won respect, riches and a reputation for valour. She had awakened their sense of duty; they were proud to be Athenians and to be descended from the heroes of old!

After the death of Cimon on the expedition against Cyprus (449 B. C.) and after the successful outcome of the peace talks during which Callias on behalf of the Athenians had negotiated a thirty-year truce with the king of the Persians at Susa, Pericles, the leader of the democratic movement at Athens, planned to rebuild the temples destroyed by the Persians not only in Athens but throughout the whole country. To this end he sent out envoys and invited the Greek cities to a pan-Hellenic congress. This scheme came to nothing because of the objections of the

448 B. C.

Lacedaemonians. Whereupon, the Athenians resolved to carry out Pericles' plans only in Athens and Attica (Plutarch: Pericles vxii).

Pericles now discussed his intentions and plans with his collaborators. Envisaged was the rich embellishment of the whole of the Acropolis. One thing was perfectly clear: the building which had first to be raised was the temple of their tutelary goddess, Athena Polias: the Parthenon.

The temple was to be in the Doric style and in marble, and to excel all others in size and splendour. Ictinus, the architect, agreed to draw up the plans, Callicrates to act as contractor for the project and Phidias, together with the best sculptors of Athens, to take care of its decoration. In reality, however, "Phidias had the overall superintendence of the building, although all the works were the creations only of front-rank artists " (Plutarch: Pericles xiii).

Construction of the Parthenon

Work on the Parthenon, the new temple of Athena Parthenos (the Virgin) on the Acropolis, began in the year 447 B. C. It was built on the highest-lying part of the hill, to the south, almost at the centre of the Acropolis. For such a big building the necessary platform had first to be created. The architects made use of the poros foundations of the earlier temple, the temple which, hardly begun, had been burnt down by the Persians. The substructure intended to adjust the level of the platform attained a depth of 35 ft towards the south-west. Only the northern section of the temple was built directly on the Acropolis rock. The new temple had roughly the same measurements as its predecessor; it was somewhat wider and not quite as long.

Just as sculptors place their works on pedestals which draw the eyes of the beholder upwards, so the ancient Greeks built their temples, the dwelling-places of divine majesty, on a raised platform or " krepis ". Since the beginning of the 6th century the Greeks had settled on the Doric style for their temples on account of its simplicity and its remarkable static qualities. " Thus, the buildings now rose to a proud height ", Plutarch (xiii) tells us, " inimitable in their beauty and nobility of form, because the craftsmen vied to surpass the original creative idea in their artistic realisation. Quite particular astonishment was aroused by the speed with which everything went forward. Of each of these buildings one would have thought it would require several generations and great efforts to build. The energy of Pericles alone inspired all and led in such short time to such flawless perfection."

And it is a fact that, during the Great Panathenaea of 438 B. C., the great temple, or simply the "ΝΑΟΣ" (Naos) as it was called (only much later did it become known as the Parthenon) was dedicated to the virginal goddess together with Phidias' ivory and gold statue of Athena Parthenos. The decoration of the pediments and the frieze was not completed until 432.

THE PARTHENON

Among all the temples built in Greece, the Parthenon stands out because of the majesty of its form, the harmony of its lines, the perfection of its architectural design, and the magnificence of its decoration with brilliant sculptures. In a word, in it we have one, if not the, crowning achievement of ancient Greek art.

It is a Doric " peripteros ", i. e. surrounded by columns: 8 columns at both the east and west ends and 17 columns along both sides, making 46 columns in all. The

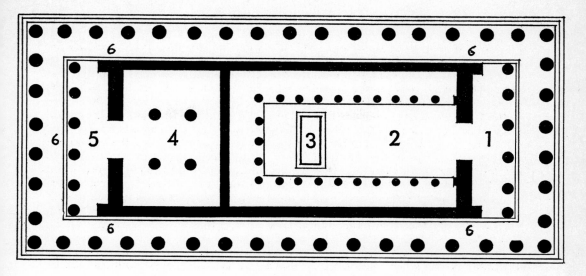

THE PARTHENON

1 Pronaos or portico   2 Sekos, cella or Hecatompedon   3 Athena Parthenos of Phidias
4 Parthenon   5 Opisthodomos (back-chamber)   6 Frieze of the Parthenon

material used was Pentelic marble. The stylobate measures 228 ft in length and
101 ft in width. Its platform (krepis), rising in three great steps, rests on the tufa
foundations of the old Parthenon. Three intermediate steps halved the height of
the three great steps at both ends of the temple and thus facilitated access to the
building. The main entrance was at the east end. Within the peristyle was the
" sekos " or cella, the temple proper, a window-less, rectangular construction some
194 ft long and 71 ft wide. There was a large door in both the east and the west
ends. Between the sekos and the 8 columns at front and back, there was another
row of 6 Doric columns, which formed an open vestibule known as the " pronaos "
in front of the east entrance to the sekos and as the " opisthodomos " in front of its
west entrance. The " sekos " itself was divided by a transverse wall into two
rooms. The eastern and larger of the two was the sanctuary in which the statue of
Athene stood; the western was known as the Parthenon and later gave its name to
the whole temple. Here all the dedicatory offerings and the temple treasure were
kept; it was also the abode of all those virgins who dedicated themselves to the
service of the goddess. In the centre of this room stood 4 Ionic columns which supported the ceiling. The larger of the two rooms, the " sekos " proper, 100 Greek
feet in length, was divided into a nave and two aisles by two rows of " double-
decker " Doric columns. The nave was much wider than the two aisles. Three further columns joined these two rows of columns at the back so that a kind of niche
(sekos) was formed in which the Athena Parthenos stood.

On entering, the visitor caught sight, deep within the temple, of Phidias' awe-
inspiring, glittering chryselephantine statue of Athena Parthenos. This work, which
had an incalculable material value in addition to its artistic worth, has unfortunately not survived. We can get a faint idea of what it must have looked like from a
small Roman copy, the Varvakeion Athene (Nat. Mus. of Athens, our Guide p. 41).
This statue by Phidias (500—432 B. C.) was the embodiment of transcendent majesty and gracious condescension. Raised on a pedestal 12 ft high, it had an overall
height of 39 ft. Athene's Attic helmet was adorned with a sphinx and two winged

The Athena
Parthenos
of Phidias

horses. The aegis with the Gorgoneion at its centre protected her breast. In her right hand she bore a winged Nike (goddess of Victory), small in comparison to Athene but nevertheless 6^1/$_2$ ft high. In her left hand she held her shield, the end of which rested on the pedestal; the outside and inside surfaces of the shield were covered with reliefs depicting the battles of the Amazons with the Athenians and of the Giants against the gods. The coiled snake which nestled against the inside of the shield represented Athene's faithful companion, Erichthonius. Her long robe, drawn in at the waist, was draped in folds evocative of column-fluting. Only the neck, arms and tips of the feet were bare. The wooden " core " of the statue was entirely covered with pure gold; even the rich drapery of her robe was overlaid with finely chased gold plate. The face and exposed parts of the body were covered with a thin layer of ivory. The birth of Pandora was depicted on the pedestal.

Architecture In building the Parthenon, Ictinus and Callicrates, the architects devised and employed a good number of architectural devices to counteract optical distortions
Architectural and impart aesthetic harmony to the whole. Thus, for example, the platform is not
Peculiarities as level as one might think, but is gently convex. The highest point of the curve is 4^1/$_2$ in. along the sides and 3^1/$_8$ in. at front and back. The same curvature is to be found in the " cross-beams resting on the columns " (the architraves).

Similarly, the 46 Doric columns are not perfectly perpendicular but incline inwards slightly towards each other and are somewhat thicker about 2/5ths of the way up, as if gathering their strength to bear the weight of the roof. The four corner-columns, too, are somewhat thicker than the others, quite contrary to appearances. The shaft of the Doric columns has 20 flutes which appear to quiver slightly in the sunlight as if some quickening ray were playing about the entire building. These Doric columns of the peristyle are built of 10 to 11 drums and, together with their capitals, attain a height of 34 ft. Their diameter at the base is a little more than 7 ft, at the top almost 5 ft.

Triglyphs The frieze of Doric temples, and thus also of the Parthenon, is made up of alter-
and nating triglyphs and metopes. Triglyphs always occupy the corner positions. A
Metopes metope, a rectangular slab covered with reliefs, comes between two triglyphs. The Parthenon had 15 triglyphs and 14 metopes along the ends, 33 triglyphs and 32 metopes along the flanks. The metopes decorating the eastern end depict scenes from the Gigantomachia, the battle between the gods, among whom we see martial Athene, and the Giants, while those of the southern flank show the battle of the Lapithae and their Athenian allies against the Centaurs. The western end bore a representation of the battle with the Amazons, the northern flank portrayed the Trojan War. The background in all the metopes was coloured red in order to make the reliefs stand out more distinctly. These reliefs were the work of various sculptors; for this reason their artistic value is not uniform.

The Parthenon was roofed with tiles of Parian marble. The double slopes of the Parthenon roof formed an isosceles triangle at the east and west ends known as the
Pediments pediment (above the horizontal cornice). These pediments were 93 ft wide, a little
of the over 11 ft high at the centre, and 3 ft thick. They were embellished with marble
Parthenon statues, for the design of which Phidias himself had been responsible from 439 to 433 B. C. The east pediment, above the entrance, depicted the birth of Athene: in the centre Zeus, seated on his throne, and at his side the new-born Athene, in full armour, portrayed in all her splendour; left and right of the two protagonists there are other gods who are spectators of the wondrous birth. In the southern angle of the pediment, the sun-god Helius is ascending on his four-horse chariot, whereas in the angle on the right the moon-goddess Selene with her four horses is making way for the orb of day.

On the west pediment, the dispute between Athene and Poseidon about the possession of Attica was depicted. In the middle, the two central figures and between them Athene's olive-tree; right and left, the gods and Athenians of early mythical times follow with sympathy and interest the victory of their goddess. Reclining in the two angles are Attic river- and spring-gods: Cephissus, Eridanus, Ilissus and the Callirrhoe Spring (cf. picture, p. 99, 100, for reconstruction of the pediment).

The Parthenon Frieze

Sculptural decoration was usual in all Doric temples, but only in the metopes of the frieze and the triangular pediments — the chief characteristic of the Doric style. In this point, the Parthenon goes its own way. It is often typical of great artists that they have the courage and the ability to break with tradition. Phidias combined the traditional with the novel in the Parthenon. He incorporated Ionian elements in the temple's otherwise uncompromising Doric severity. And the courage required to make such a combination not only did not impair the overall concept, but was rather regarded as its indispensable completion. The stylistic departure consisted in a frieze 525 ft long and 3½ ft high which ran without interruption around the entire naos fairly high up within the peristyle. The reliefs of this frieze depict the Panathenaic procession. Thus, the subject matter was not drawn from the mythology of the gods or from the legends of the heroes, as was usual for the decoration of temples, but both these spheres are reflected in the representation of the solemn procession as the Athenians of the 5th century knew it. The entire procession is reproduced on the frieze by means of particularly characteristic scenes. It unfolds before the eyes of the beholder and encircles the entire shrine. The procession moves off in two directions from the south-western corner of the Parthenon. The one group passes along the western and then the northern walls of the temple, the other processes in the opposite direction. The two meet on the eastern wall, above the entrance to the temple. On the eastern side we see gods on their thrones, respectful " ergastinae " giving the peplus they have woven to the priestess of Athene, maidens with baskets of flowers and others from the head of the procession with their gifts. The other participants are still on their way. Young people with their animals, lambs and oxen, from which a hecatomb (100 oxen) was offered to the goddess, the tray-bearers, flutists, pitcher-carriers, the group of citizens with olive branches, between them an official directing the procession near the charioteers and one of the " apobatae ", finally the long cavalcade which occupies the entire western wall and beginning of the southern and northern walls. In the south-west corner, the viewer could see the preparations the youthful riders are making, could see them bridling, curbing and mounting their horses with expert ease. Then they take their place in the procession, and move off in pairs, following the others, towards the eastern end of the temple. In this representation of the Panathenaic procession, the artist depicts many scenes which reflect how live was the interest and how active the participation of his fellow citizens. From all these individual scenes he created a coherent, incomparable work of art, an everlasting paean of praise to the goddess Athene.

Death of Phidias 432 B. C.

Envious enemies of Pericles turned against his friend Phidias and accused him of converting to his own personal advantage some of the gold entrusted to him for the statue of Athena Parthenos. He was easily able to refute this charge by weighing the golden robe of the goddess before their eyes (some 23 cwt!). Later, they reproached him for including portraits of himself and his friend Pericles on Athene's shield. This was considered impious. Phidias was thrown into prison, where he fell ill and died in the same year (432 B. C.) as his sculptures for the Parthenon were completed and admired by all (Plutarch: Pericles xxxi).

THE PROPYLAEA

Work was begun on the Propylaea in the year 437 B. C., after the completion of the Parthenon. A start could not be made earlier, partly because the architect and craftsmen were still engaged on the Parthenon and partly because the enormous marble blocks required for the temple could only be conveyed to the building-site through this one entrance to the Acropolis. The Propylaea would have made the transport of this material difficult.

Pericles had commissioned the architect Mnesicles to draw up the plans for the monumental gateway. Mnesicles wanted the Propylaea to rival the Parthenon, so that he envisaged an imposing construction which was to occupy the entire western side of the Acropolis. But this plan could not be realised because of the stubborn resistance of the priests and the opposition of the conservative-minded. Mnesicles' original plans necessitated the destruction of, or detriment to, older sanctuaries. The sanctuaries involved were that of the Graces, which adjoined the Artemis Brauronia, and that of the Athena Nike in the south-west. The original plans had therefore to be altered and the building reduced in size. This modified project was completed in all essentials within a period of 5 years.

The Propylaea was built of Pentelic marble and consisted of a central construction and two projecting wings on the south-west and north-west sides. This central construction occupied the site of the earlier Pisistratid propylaeum and stood on a rectangular platform of large dimensions. It was walled on the north and south sides, and was open on the eastern side, i. e. that facing the Acropolis, and on the western side. This central building was subdivided into two by a transverse wall, the western section being twice as large as the eastern. This transverse wall was pierced by five heavy wooden doors with metal fittings; the door in the centre was the widest ($13^2/_3$ ft), the two on either side being smaller ($9^5/_6$ ft and some $4^3/_4$ ft). The façade of the western portico had six Doric columns, of which the two in the centre were spaced to correspond in width with the central opening in the transverse wall. Two rows of 3 slim Ionic columns then ranged in line with these two central columns of the façade and divided the intervening space into three. The wider, middle intercolumniation formed the access way for processions, sacrificial animals and chariots, and was inclined, without steps, in contrast to the passageway on either side. Here the krepis was provided with 4 marble steps at the western end and with 5 between the 2 porticos. The Ionic columns supported the ceiling of the great stoa; the ceiling was decorated with marble-tiled coffers with gilded stars on a blue background. The small eastern portico was also a Doric hexastyle. Here the floor is 5 ft higher than in the western and larger portico; this accounts for the great number of marble steps. Both porticos had a frieze and a pediment above the architrave but without decoration. The north wing consisted of a rectangular hall ($35^1/_2$ ft $\times$ $29^1/_2$ ft) and a vestibule with 3 Doric columns in antis towards the south. These were smaller than those of the adjoining western portico. A door and two windows in the wall between the hall and the vestibule admitted light into the room which was known as the Pinacotheca. Pausanias who visited the Acropolis nearly 600 years later tells us how he admired the frescoes and large paintings by Polygnotus there (Pausanias: Attica xxii, 6). This shows they were still there to be seen in his day. Offsetting the Pinacotheca was the southern wing of the Propylaea, a vestibule open to north and west, but closed on the other two sides. 3 Doric columns likewise adorned its front. The south wing was not as large as the northern, because, as we have already pointed out above, respect for older buildings necessitated this. The vestibule opened onto the terrace of the temple of Athena Nike.

TEMPLE OF ATHENA NIKE

The temple of Athena Nike was built on the western part of the Acropolis, on the site where a bastion had stood in Mycenaean times to defend the entrance to the sacred hill. During the time of the Pisitratids, a small temple and altar had been raised here dedicated to Athena Nike. But this, too, had been destroyed by the Persians in 480 B. C. along with the other shrines and sanctuaries. Immediately after their victory over the Persians at the naval battle of Salamis, the Athenians had raised an altar (478 B. C.) and had then decided about the year 448 B. C. to dedicate a temple to Athena Nike.

A levelling course of symmetrical, smooth-cut poros blocks was first laid. This created a wider, raised foundation which covered the older sanctuaries. The construction of the actual temple, however, was not started until the Parthenon and the Propylaea were finished (c. 432 B. C.). Callicrates was the architect in charge of the project. The small temple he designed was built of Pentelic marble in the Ionic style and was an " amphiprostyle-tetrastyle ", i. e. the " pronaos " and the " opisthodomus " were formed by a row of four columns.

Thus there arose in the western corner of the Acropolis, on the site of the ancient bastion, the ethereal Ionian temple of Athena Nike, delicately poised on its socle, in thanksgiving for the many victories which their tutelary goddess had granted the Athenians against the Persians. The temple rested on a three-tiered platform and consisted of the sekos or cella, the shrine in which the cult image of the goddess stood. This was a copy of the ancient xoanon. Athene held in her right hand a pomegranate as a symbol of fertility and in her left her helmet. This statue of Athena Nike (Nike = goddess of Victory) was, in contrast to the other Nike images, wingless. This gave rise to the legend that the Athenians had cut off the wings of Nike so that she should remain with them forever. The cella of the temple was open to the east and had two square columns in antis with a grill between to enclose the cella. 4 monolithic Ionic columns at both the east and the west end supported the architrave. An 82-ft-long Ionic frieze decorated with plastic representations adorned the entire circumference of the temple: on the eastern façade an assembly of the Olympian gods with Zeus, Athene and Poseidon in the centre, on the northern and southern walls scenes from the battles with the Persians and on the west front the battle of Plataea (479 B. C.). The pediments were also filled with sculptural decoration.

The altar stood in front of the temple. The terrace was paved. However, because the temple stood at the westernmost edge of the " pyrgos " (ancient fortification) and there was danger that the visitors might fall to their deaths, a parapet was built along three sides at the edge of the pyrgos, with marble tablets on its external face. These tablets, almost $3^{1}/_{2}$ ft high, attained a length of $133^{1}/_{2}$ ft, when placed side to side, as they were along the edge of the pyrgos. They depicted Athene enthroned who received the homage of the beautiful winged Nikes (goddesses of Victory). One makes ready for the sacrifice, another approaches with her finest calf, others set up trophies, and the most famous in her richly draped, form-hugging robe loosens her sandals to enter the temple barefoot.

These tablets were affixed to the parapet around the pyrgos about 411—407 B. C. The winged Nikes were intended to extol the victories of Alcibiades which raised the Athenian hopes of a successful outcome to the war against Sparta. But by 404 B. C. the defeat of the Athenians was already sealed.

THE ERECHTHEUM

Among the plans which Pericles drew up with his advisers for the splendid re-construction of the Acropolis was also one for an entirely new temple on the site where that of Athena Polias and Poseidon had formerly stood, i. e. to replace the " Erechtheum " burnt down by the Persians in 480 B. C. This new temple was to house the wooden cult image of Athene which had found a temporary and make-shift home elsewhere; at the same time it was to enclose within its wall other relics of the pious faith of their forefathers: the marks of Poseidon's trident, the salt spring, Athene's sacred olive tree, altars of the gods and heroes, and the tomb of Cecrops. Work was to have begun on the Erechtheum after the Parthenon, Propylaea and the temple of Athena Nike had been completed. However, the outbreak of the Pe-loponnesian War delayed the start. Building could only commence in c. 421 after the peace treaty which the Athenian Nicias concluded with the Spartans. Pericles, the great leader of the Athenians, did not live to see this. He had died in September 429 as a victim of the frightful plague epidemic which had ravaged Athens in 430. With his death, the " Golden Age of Pericles " also came to a close.

The name of the architect who designed the Erechtheum has not come down to us. All we know is that in the last two years it was a-building, the supervision of the work lay in the hands of the architect Philicles. The original plans, however, do not appear to have been carried out in their entirety. Probably the temple should have extended further west and have been rounded off on this side, too, by another porch.

After the two imposing Doric buildings, the Parthenon and the Propylaea, the ar-chitect of the Erechtheum sought his inspiration in the Ionic style. The contrast is interesting, especially if one bears in mind the rich variety of forms which this style has to offer. The Erechtheum was worthy to stand alongside the Parthenon: the aim here was not majestic grandeur but delicate and subtle harmony. Before he could translate his plan into reality, the architect had two important problems to solve: the ground on which he was to build inclined sharply from east to west and from south to north; further, this temple had to enclose, and yet leave acces-sible for the veneration of the faithful, all the ancient cultic relics: the marks of Poseidon's Trident, the " Sea of Erechtheus " with its salt water, and so on. But all of these were located on the northern side and therefore at a much lower level than the east and south sides. For this reason the building conforms to the irregu-larities of the ground-surface. The groundplan of the Erechtheum is a large rectan-gle (approx. 79 ft × 44 ft) with three porches, one each on the north, east and south sides. The interior was divided by a cross-wall into rooms. The eastern, dedicated to Athena Polias, housed her cult statue. According to Pausanias, a golden lamp, the work of Callimachus, burnt here day and night; it was filled but once a year and its wick never burnt out. A palm tree in bronze rose up over the lamp as high as the ceiling and drew off the smoke. The entrance to this sanctuary, the cella of Athene, was in the east porch, where a window pierced each of the side walls. This porch had 6 Ionic columns resting on a stylobate of three steps which ran round the whole length of the south flank.

The Cella of Athena Polias

The visitor entered the cella of Poseidon in the western part of the Erechtheum from the north side, which was at a level some 10 ft lower than the eastern. A broad external stairway with 12 steps led from the east side down to the north porch, which formed a " pronaos " (34 ft × 22 ft) in front of the great entrance door (14½ × 6½ ft). Four Ionic columns adorned its façade and there was a return of one further column on each side, all resting again on a stylobate of three steps.

The Cella of Poseidon and Erechtheus

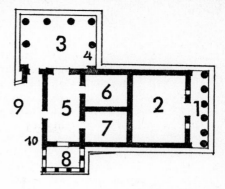

ERECHTHEION

1 Eastern portico 2 Cella of Athena Polias
3 Northern portico 4 Marks of Poseidon's
trident   5 Prostomiaion and under it the
Erechthean sea 6 Altar of Poseidon and
Erechtheus 7 Altars of Hephaestus and of
the hero Butes   8 Hall of the Caryatides
9 Pandroseum 10 Tomb of Cecrops

This ran round the north side of the temple like a cornice. As was usual in the Ionic order, the shaft of these 6 columns had 24 flutings. The top rim of the bases was decorated with a tress ornament. Under the volutes of the capitals were palmettes and egg-and-dart moulding. The three gently overlapping marble fascia of the architrave were crowned by a continuous frieze in blue Eleusinian marble which encircled the entire temple; this frieze formed an effective background for the marble figures which were affixed to it.

The frieze, if we count that of the north porch too, was not far short of 300 ft in length. On it were depicted scenes from Attic mythology and from the temple rites and worship. It appears that Creusa at Delphi with her husband Xuthus and her son Ion was to be seen on the east side of the north porch (Euripides: Ion), the birth of Erichthonius on the façade, and a chariot and horses, the invention of Erichthonius, on the south side, as well as much more besides. But none of the plastic decoration was up to the standard of the works of Phidias on the Parthenon frieze (and anyway they have survived only in a very damaged state). The coffers of the ceiling were in blue and decorated with golden stars. Through an opening in the ceiling known as the " opaion " one could see the blue sky above. Immediately below this were the marks of Poseidon's trident in the bare rock.

According to Pausanias, the altar of " Zeus Hypatos ", of " Supreme Zeus ", stood in this porch in front of the entrance. To the right of the large portal there was a smaller door which gave access to the Pandroseum, in which Athene's sacred olive tree grew. The great doorway, the main entrance to the Erechtheum, was richly adorned in the Ionic style, truly a chef-d'œuvre of Attic art. It led to the western section of the temple, which was divided into three. Its groundplan formed a large rectangle. The first, oblong room extended as far as the south wall and was called the " prostomiaion ". It had a " mouth ", or opening in the floor at the bottom of which the " Sea of Erechtheus ", of which Pausanias speaks, could be seen. The adjoining rectangular room to the east was divided into two by a cross-wall. In Pausanias we read: " In the Erechtheum there are several altars, one for Poseidon where the Athenians, in obedience to an oracle, also sacrifice to Erechtheus, another for the hero Butes and a third for Hephaestus. Pictures of the priestly family of the Butadae adorn the walls. Noteworthy here is the spring of salt water from which one can hear the sound of waves when the wind blows from the south. "

Along the west front, 4 Ionic columns stood on a base wall 12 ft high between antae. Wooden trellis-work enclosed the space between the columns. A small door in the middle of this wall led to the Pandroseum. In the south-west corner of the Erechtheum there was the tomb of Cecrops under a great marble slab.

The monotony of the south wall is broken by the Porch of the Maidens or Caryatids which was built into the south-west corner of the Erechtheum in 415 B. C. Here the roof is supported by figures of maidens or kores instead of columns. The caryatids stand on a course of marble orthostates; the pedestal immediately be-

The Porch of
the Maidens

31

neath their feet is decorated with egg-and-dart moulding. Four of these kores graced the porch front; there was an extra one on both sides. The three of the eastern half bend their right knee, the other three their left. The long peplus, caught up at the waist, reached down to their feet and hugged their figures in rich folds. The perpendicular folds falling down the erect leg are reminiscent of column fluting. In spite of the weight they are bearing on their heads, their posture is proud and noble. Their hair, falling down in thick tresses at the back, imparts still greater static strength to neck. On their heads they bear baskets decorated with egg-and-art moulding which support the ceiling beams. These consisted of the architrave and the richly decorated cornice. The ceiling itself was likewise embellished with coffers in marble. An opening in the east wall and eleven steps led down to the " prostomiaion " of the Erechtheum.

At first the Caryatids were directly opposite the western part of the temple of Athena Polias which had been built during the years the Pisistratidae were in power. After the Persian conflagration on the Acropolis (480 B. C.), the Athenians, out of awe and reverence, had not torn down what still stood of this temple but had restored it as best they could. The cult image of Athene found a temporary home there. But, in 406 B. C., the temple was completely destroyed by a fire that was perhaps not accidental. (Xenophon: Hellenica I, vi). The south-west corner of the Erechtheum was also damaged by this fire. When the gutted ruins had been cleared, the people had an unhindered view of the grace and beauty of the Erechtheum.

OTHER SHRINES AND SANCTUARIES ON THE ACROPOLIS

The sacred hill was not only adorned by the magnificent buildings we have described above: the Parthenon, the Erechtheum, the Propylaea and the temple of Athena Nike. There were other sanctuaries as well, and above all an abundance of votive offerings in the form of statues. These lined the Sacred Way and lent an air of festive beauty to the open spaces on the Acropolis as a token of the pious reverence of their donors. South-east of the Propylaea was the open-air

The Temenos of Artemis Brauronia

sanctuary of Artemis Brauronia. This temenos included two pillared halls, a longish one to the south and a smaller one to the east. The larger of the two was subdivided: the one room housed the ancient cult image of Artemis, the other the splendid statue of the goddess executed by Praxiteles.

Athena Ergane

East of this precinct, in the direction of the Parthenon, there was, on a raised terrace, the temenos of Athena Ergane, to whom artisans and their wives brought their offerings.

The Chalcotheke

In the background was the Chalcotheke, a narrow rectangular building along the Wall of Cimon. Here ancient bronze weapons were stored. A stoa and a colonnade adorned its front.

East of the Temenos of Athena Ergane, 8 steps cut in the steep rock led up to the terrace of the Parthenon. 38 votive stelae with reliefs and inscriptions stood on these steps.

The altar and statue of " Gaea Carpophorus ", " Fruit-bringing Earth ", was roofless: the Earth-goddess addresses her petitions to Zeus, the " Rain-Giver ". This sanctuary stood about half way between the centre of the northern foundation of the Parthenon and the Sacred Way.

The Shrine of Zeus Polieus, " Protector of the city ", was situated on the highest point of the Acropolis, to the north-east of the Parthenon (cf. plan, pp. 8/9, No. 18).

The great altar of Athene, on the other hand, on which during the Panathenaic Festival whole hecatombs were sacrificed, lay to the east between the Erechtheum and the Parthenon (cf. plan, pp. 8/9, No. 15). To the west (and near the Erechtheum) was the Pandroseum. There was probably a small temple of Pandrosos here; within the precincts of this sanctuary was also located the sacred olive tree of Athene and an altar of Zeus " Herceius ", the " Protector ".

The Pandroseum

Further west of the Erechtheum was the house of the Arrephoroi, near the north wall (cf. plan, pp. 8/9, No. 11).

Of the many statues adorning the open spaces of the Acropolis, Phidias' Athena Promachus or, as the Athenians themselves called it, the Bronze Athene, was the most impressive, alone on account of its size. The work was solemnly dedicated c. 454 B. C. after the conclusion of the Persian Wars, some years before work began on the Parthenon. This bronze colossus, the first Athene executed by Phidias, was 29 ft high including the socle (5 ft) and stood between the Propylaea and the temple of Athena Polias, to the left of the Sacred Way. The goddess was represented in full armour. Helmeted, she held her shield in her left hand and her spear in her right. We are told that sailors, when they rounded Cape Sunium to enter the bay of Phaleron, could already see in the distance the plumed crest of her helmet and the golden tip of her spear. On the inside of the shield of the Athena Promachus the battle between the Lapiths and the Centaurs was depicted; this was the work of the famous silversmith Mys after a sketch of the celebrated painter Parrhasius. Both belong to a generation after Phidias. The Lemnian Athene, likewise a work of Phidias, showed Athene as the goddess of peace. She was represented without helmet, shield or spear. Attic settlers on the island of Lemnos dedicated the bronze statue to Athene as the patroness of peace.

The Athena Promachus

The Lemnian Athene

In the south-east corner of the Propylaea, near the goddess' earlier altar, was the bronze statue of Athena " Hygieia " (Health) by Pyrrhus, which was dedicated in 430 B. C. This statue was a thank-offering for a revelation made to Pericles in a dream in which he was shown a cure for one of his best workmen who had fallen from a great height while working on the Propylaea.

The Athena Hygieia

The sacred precincts of the Acropolis were remarkable not only for these statues by Phidias, but for the works of many other artists also represented there. Pausanias, who visited the Acropolis in the second century after Christ, was " dazzled " by the profusion of works of art which he saw there. He mentions more than 65 statues and plastic groups, each of them with the name of the artist responsible. Among them are: the Hermes Propylaeus by Alcamenes near the entrance to the Propylaea, Procne with her son Itys, likewise by Alcamenes and standing north-east of the Parthenon, the Aphrodite by Calamis, the Charites by Socrates, Perseus by Myron, Zeus by Leochares, and the Trojan Horse by Stongylion. All these temples, monuments and works of art which embellished the sacred rock of the Acropolis were built within a period of a bare half century. They represent an era in which the soaring aspirations of the human spirit and the creative urge for artistic expression have left eloquent testimony to the greatness of Classical Greece. It was, for this reason, later called the Golden Age of Greece.

Pericles, in his genius, had conjured up a vision of an Acropolis crowded with mighty and immortal works of architecture and art. He himself did not live to see the fulfilment of his plans. But his collaborators, spurred on by his creative example, brought to final perfection what he was not spared to see. The result was an Acropolis formed by beauty and lavish harmony. And since the other fields of cultural endeavour, especially the sciences, attained the same peaks as art and literature, the Acropolis and its environs soon developed into the intellectual centre of Greece. Athens cast a bright light over Greece, over the West — which was especially formed by it —, indeed over the whole globe.

The reconstruction programme for the Acropolis had been completed in all essentials by c. 400 B. C.

Athena Polias was reverenced down to the Byzantine Period. But the faith which had been so living during the 5th century B. C. began to grow cold. The teachings of many philosophers and the disillusioning theories of numerous Sophists shook the Athenian's faith in his great protectress. And Attic art, which had scaled Olympian heights, also succumbed to the spirit of the age; instead of singing the praises of the divine Government of the world, the art of Attica became the handmaid of the mighty and created their images.

But for all that, every age has left its mark on the Acropolis. After his victory at the River Granicus, Alexander the Great, for instance, sent helmets of bronze gilt to the goddess as an ex voto. They were affixed to both façades of the Parthenon, 14 to the east front and 8 to the west (the holes in the architrave of the east façade, cf. Plate 20, show where they hung). Lachares, tyrant of Athens, took these helmets and the gold jewels of the chryselephantine statue of Athena with him to Boeotia in 298 B. C.

The fame of the greatness and wealth of Athens and Greece, which was carried to " the ends of the world ", aroused the envy and greed of numerous peoples who poured into Greek territory in ever renewed waves and conquered all: Romans, Goths, Byzantines, Slavs, Franks, Catalans, Florentines, Venetians and Turks.

The Roman Period 146 B. C.—395 A. D. The Romans, who occupied Greece from 146 B. C. to 395 A. D., carried off a great number of statues. Sulla and Nero alone brought more than 3500 works of plastic art back to Rome with them from Greece to beautify their palaces and dwellings. In contrast, the Emperor Hadrian and Herodes Atticus enriched Athens with many splendid buildings.

The fate of Athens was thus dependent on the good or bad will of the respective emperor and governor.

Temple of Rome and Augustus The Romans spared the Acropolis monuments. They added an Ionic rotunda with a peristyle of 9 columns which they dedicated to the goddess Rome and Augustus.

To the north of the Propylaea entrance, a statue in honour of Agrippa, the son-in-law of Augustus, was raised on a marble socle 29 ft high.

During the reign of Caligula (40 A. D.), the Romans built a magnificent monumental stairway which took in the whole width in front of the entrance to the Propylaea from the monument of Agrippa to the pyrgos of the temple of Athena Nike. The central section without steps was laid out as a road wide enough (11½ ft) to accommodate the sacrificial animals. During the reign of Hadrian, c. 120 A. D., the beginning of this way was flanked by two towers of purely decorative character. Shortly before 161 A. D., Herodes Atticus built, on the southern slope of the Acropolis, the Odeum with its tiers of marble seats (cf. Plates 2 and 7).

At the beginning of the 4th century after Christ, the Roman emperor Constantine the Great, who had moved his capital to Byzantium, proclaimed his new-found Christian faith the State religion.

By this time, Athens had already lost everything of its former splendour and glory. Now it was nothing more than un unimportant provincial town. Certainly, until this time, the monuments on the Acropolis had suffered little, but nothing remained of the magnificent cultic festivals of earlier times. The Acropolis was now regarded as a sort of museum of art and not as the residence of the gods to whom prayers, sacrifices and votive gifts were offered.

About the year 435 A. D., the Emperor Theodosius II outlawed the worship of the ancient gods. As a consequence the Athena Promachus was removed from the Acropolis; of its fate thereafter we know nothing. The Athena Parthenos, too, was carried off to Constantinople (Byzantium).

Since the days of Pericles, the Athenians had rendered the Acropolis monuments their due in admiration and reverence. Nor did they ever cease to regard them as memorials to the pious faith of their forefathers and as surpassing works of art. This explains why, when the Athenians adopted Christianity, they never tore these monuments down, but transformed them into Christian churches.

Thus, the interior of the Parthenon was transformed into a Christian Church. Its entrance was at the west end. The transverse wall which had divided the sanctuary into cella and Parthenon was pierced by three doors; the ceiling was vaulted, the walls covered with frescoes of Christian saints. Externally it remained the Parthenon of yore. The church was at first dedicated to the " Wisdom of God " (Hagia Sophia); later it was renamed the " Panagia Atheniotissa ".

The Erechtheum, too, was transformed into a church under the title " Panagia Theotokos " (All-Holy Mother of God).

The only really festal days which Athens and the Acropolis saw during the whole of the Byzantine Period were celebrated when the Emperor Basil II, after defeating the Bulgarians, who had invaded Greece, came down with his army from Thessaly to Athens to thank the Panagia Atheniotissa for his victories.

When the Latin crusaders took Constantinople in 1204 A. D., the Frank Othon de la Roche came to Athens, entitled himself " Great Lord of Athens " and took up residence with his entire retinue on the Acropolis, which was now fortified like a citadel. During the period of Frankish domination, the Acropolis once again became the focal point of Athens. Some alterations were made to the Parthenon church, which became the church of " Santa Maria di Atene " (1209). Frankish Occupation

The Catalans succeeded the Franks as lords of Athens and the Acropolis (1311-87). The Catalans They founded a Spanish duchy there. But the Catalans were expelled in their turn in 1387 by the Florentines under Nerio Acciajuoli. Acciajuoli set up his palace in The Florentines the Propylaea, to the south side of which he added a square tower 85 ft high. In the year 1458, the citadel's garrison was compelled to surrender to the Turks, who had conquered Constantinople some years before. In 1466, the Turks transformed The Turks the Parthenon into a mosque topped with a minaret. The Turkish governor, Disdar, quartered his harem in the Erechtheum.

The Turkish occupation, which lasted 375 years, was to wreak the greatest havoc on the Acropolis monuments, which until this time had preserved their essential form. The mischief began in 1656 when lightning struck the powder magazine which 1656 the Turks had set up in the Propylaea. The central hall was shattered by the explosion. The Turks then pulled down the temple of Athena Nike, which until the year 1687 had stood undamaged on its pyrgos. This act of vandalism supplied the building material needed to transform the Propylaea into a fortified stronghold. The open space thus created served as the site for the Turkish cannonry which bombarded the besieging army of the Doge of Venice, Francesco Morosini.

On 7 o'clock of a September evening in 1687, a Venetian bomb hit the Parthenon. Sept. 1687 Serious Damage to the Parthenon: Morosini Here, in their mosque, the Turks had again set up a gunpowder magazine. The entire building was shaken by the explosion. The interior walls of the cella collapsed and, in falling, brought some three quarters of the frieze down with them. 28 columns on the north and south sides crashed down. The catastrophe was to be sealed by the hand of man. The Doge Francesco Morosini wanted to take the central section of the west pediment depicting the dispute between Athene and Poseidon back to Venice with him as a trophy of his great deed. The Venetians went about their work so clumsily, that the debris of this great work of art strew the ground.

The First Tourists on the Acropolis About the year 1436 and therefore before the Turkish conquest, Cyriac of Ancona, who visited the Acropolis on his travels, was the first to recognise the " temple of Pallas Athene " in the Church of Santa Maria di Atene. He made a drawing of it. His accompanying notes reflect his delight in all that met his eyes.

From the 16th to the 17th century and particularly during the 18th century, many foreigners, admirers of Classical Greece, began to visit Athens and the Acropolis. A number of them have left admiring descriptions of the monuments; others, like Jacques Carrey in 1674, have sketched the plastic art of the Parthenon. Their accounts and sketches are of great value to us for they give us an idea of the state of the monuments before the catastrophe.

After the work of destruction of 1687, the foreign visitors were often no longer satisfied with admiring and drawing the works of art, but frequently took some piece of sculpted marble home with them as a genuine souvenir of their visit.

Thus, le Comte de Choiseul-Gouffier was able, with the aid of the French Consul in Athens, M. Fauvel, to take back to France a portion of the frieze and two metopes which he had rescued from the debris.

Lord Elgin The Scottish peer, Lord Elgin, was the man who sinned most grievously against the Greek temples in this respect. Armed with a firman from the Sultan which permitted him to remove " some stone blocks with inscriptions and figures " he ascended the Acropolis with some workmen under the supervision of the painter Lusieri and stripped the Parthenon almost entirely of its plastic decoration: 12 statues, 56 panels from the freize, 15 metopes, a Caryatid and a column from the north-east side of the Erechtheum as well as parts of the temple of Athena Nike. This was the harvest of the plunder which he proudly brought back to London with him and sold to the British government for Pound 35,000 (1816). These " Elgin Marbles " are now on view in the British Museum.

Twelve years after the Greek revolution (1821), the Turks were forced to abandon the Acropolis after withstanding repeated sieges. A year later, Athens was declared the capital of Greece, which had been pronounced a monarchy. Otto of the Bavarian House of Wittelsbach ascended the throne. Shortly afterwards the first excavations were carried out on the Acropolis under the archaeologist K. Pittakis working with numerous foreign colleagues. The first task undertaken was the removal of all later accretions to the monuments of the excavations and the restoration of the buildings since then.

The extensive excavations carried out under the leadership of the archaeologist P. Kavadia lasted from 1885 to 1891. They brought precious finds to light, among which were also the foundations of the until-then-unknown temple of Athena Polias between the Parthenon and the Erechtheum. 14 kores, on which the light of the sun played for the first time again after some two and a half millenia, were uncovered north of the Erechtheum.

In the area south of the Parthenon, the terrace, a variety of sculptured poros came to light, marble statues and separate architectural parts of temples or other buildings. The temple of the " Wingless Athene " was almost entirely rebuilt from the original parts which were rediscovered when the fortifications of the Propylaea were carefully dismantled.

About 1852/53, the French archaeologist Ernest Beulé dug west of the Propylaea. Between the two towers from Roman times he found a marble gateway which has since then been known, in his honour, as the Beulé gate.

In 1875, Heinrich Schliemann bore the costs of having the Frankish tower inside the Propylaea pulled down.

The great restorations of the Propylaea, the Erechtheum and the Parthenon were carried out under the architect N. Balanos.

The poros and marble sculptures which had been unearthed during the numerous excavations on the Acropolis were housed from 1874 until after World War II in the old Acropolis Museum.

Since that time they have found a new home in the present Acropolis Museum, a new building for whose up-to-date layout and arrangement the director, Jannis Miliadis, and his collaborators, K. Mulos, D. Demetriades and D. Perrakis, were responsible.

The scientific study of the old and new finds and of the Acropolis monuments, which all bear the marks of their eventful history, still continues. They are not only able to advance the viewer's knowledge of the past, however, they can inspire every open-minded visitor with something of that enthusiasm and reverent gratitude without which they would never have been raised. Thus, they continue to show their vitality as the spring that will never run dry!

EXPLANATORY NOTES TO THE PLATES

1	View of the south-east face of the Acropolis taken from the Temple of Zeus Olympius. In the foreground two Corinthian columns of this temple.
2	The south-west face of the Acropolis, from Museum Hill, present-day Philopappos. At the top, from left to right, we see: the socle of the Agrippa monument, the Propylaea, the temple of Athena Nike on its pyrgos, in the centre the Erechtheum and the Parthenon (west and south sides). In the right-hand corner and hardly visible, the Museum. From here one can admire Cimon's Wall (built c. 468 B. C.) almost in its entirety. Bottom, the Odeum of Herodes Atticus and, further to the right, the Stoa of Eumenes.
3	The Acropolis as seen from Piraeus, the harbour of Athens. Distance: 6 1/2 miles.
4	The north-west face of the Acropolis viewed from the Areopagus (where the supreme court met in ancient Greece and the Apostle Paul preached his famous sermon to the Athenians). From this standpoint, we can see why the Acropolis was such a secure citadel.
5	The Acropolis by night.
6	View of the west face of the Acropolis.
7	Panoramic view of Athens from the Acropolis, with the sea in the distance. In the foreground at the foot of the Acropolis: the Odeum of Herodes Atticus, Philopappos Hill, and the bay of Phaleron. In the left background: the mountains of the island of Aegina, then those of the Peloponnese, and, to the right, those of Salamis with the famous narrow channel separating the island from the mainland.
8	Coloured panoramic view of the Acropolis, west face, taken from Pnyx Hill (place of public assembly in ancient Athens). To the left of the Acropolis, we see the low rocky hill of the Areopagus. In the background, Mt Hymettus, which, in the light of the setting sun, looks as if it's " crowned with violets " (Pindar: Ἀθῆναι ἰοστέφανοι).
9	Temple of Athena Nike or of Apteros Nike (Wingless Victory) from the west (cf. Plates 111, 112, 114, and text p. 29). The broad stairway leads up to the entrance of the Propylaea and the Acropolis. Top left, the south wing of the Propylaea.
10	The Propylaea, east portico. Mnesicles was the architect of the Propylaea, which was built of Pentelic marble in the Doric style between the years 437—432 B. C. It forms the monumental entrance to the Acropolis (cf. text, p. 28).

The transverse wall with its 5 doorways can be seen through the 6 Doric columns of the front. The widest opening in the centre was to allow the Panathenaic festival procession to pass through. The distance between the two central Doric columns is wider for this reason, too. In the background, to the right, the east wall of the Pinacotheca.

11   Entrance to the temple of Athena Nike, east front. This temple was built by Callicrates entirely of Pentelic marble in c. 432 B. C. The stylobate is 27 ft long and 18 ft wide. The columns, including the base and capital, are 13 ft high. (For further details cf. text, p. 29). The frieze, although severely damaged, has survived, but only the east and south sections are to be seen in situ. The other two sides were taken to London by Lord Elgin. They have been replaced on the Acropolis by cement copies.

12   The Propylaea. The interior of the central building.

13   One of the six Ionic columns which lined both sides of the Sacred Way in the interior of the west portico.

14   Remains of the Pisistratid Propylaeum (6th century B. C.): three steps and part of a wall, which can be seen inside the Propylaea in the south-east corner (Cf. text, p. 16 and Plan, p. 8/9, No. 6).

15   The Parthenon, seen from the east portico of the Propylaea.

15—26 28 29 The Parthenon: Doric temple dedicated to Athena Parthenos built entirely of Pentelic marble, c. 447—438 B. C., i. e. under Pericles. Ictinus and Callicrates were the architects. The entire plastic decoration of the temple was executed under the direction of Phidias, the great sculptor (for further details, cf. text, pp. 24—27).

16   The Parthenon and a part of the Propylaea on the right side.

17   Parthenon interior, east end.

18   Parthenon interior. The " sekos " or cella, looking west. In the centre some raised stones on which the statue of Athena Parthenos stood (cf. text, pp. 25/26).

19   The Parthenon, from the north-east.

20   Parthenon: details from the sculptures of the metope and the east pediment. This pediment depicted the wondrous birth of Athene. In the angle on the left, Helius with his four horses, on the right the heads of the moon-goddess Selene's horses (cf. text, pp. 26/27 and the reconstruction of the pediments, Plates 99 and 100). Most of the figures still surviving on the east pediment and some from the west pediment were taken to London by Lord Elgin in 1803. They are now on view in the British Museum. The figures which we see today on the east pediment of the Parthenon are, most of them, copies. The holes in the architrave were for the gilded shields, a votive offering of Alexander the Great (cf. text, p. 34).

21   The Parthenon, from the north-west. On this picture the external frieze over the architrave, consisting of alternating triglyphs and metopes, can easily be seen. Below the triglyphs, " drops " form a decorative motif. The Parthenon had a total of 92 metopes, of which only 42, in a badly damaged state, still adorn the Parthenon. One metope is to be seen in the Acropolis Museum. 15 metopes from the south side were carried off to London, and 1 to Paris. Of the 19—21 figures which composed the scene probably depicting the dispute between Athena and Poseidon on the west pediment (cf. text, p. 27) only two extremely damaged figures (perhaps Cecrops and his daugther Pandrosos) are still in situ.

22—25   The famous frieze of the Parthenon, the work of Phidias and his collaborators, depicted the procession of the Panathenaic festival. From the frieze on the west wall, four details which are still in situ. The rider is ready to join the procession (cf. text, p. 27). The largest part of this frieze was carried off to London by Lord Elgin, where it is now to be seen in the British Museum. On the Parthenon, almost the whole west frieze is still in situ, 13 panels, and on the south-west wall, 3 very damaged panels. 20 panels are on view in the Acropolis Museum (Room VIII). One very fine panel from the east wall is in the Louvre, Paris.

26   The Parthenon from the east.

27, 30—33	The Erechtheum. The Erechtheum, a temple in the Ionic style dedicated to Athena Polias and Poseidon-Erechtheus, built of Pentelic marble during the period 421—406 B. C. (For description cf. text, pp. 30—32).
27	The Erechtheum: left the southern flank with the Porch of the Maidens or of the Caryatids, right the east porch, the entrance to the cella of Athena Polias. The stones and marble debris on the left lie where formerly the Pisistratid temple of Athena Polias stood. In the left-hand corner, the tufa base of a wooden column which was part of the megaron of the palace of ancient Mycenaean times.
28	Parthenon interior, north-east corner, after rain.
29	The colonnade along the south flank of the Parthenon, looking east.
30	The Porch of the Maidens or of the Caryatids (cf. text, pp. 31, 32). The second Caryatid from the left is only a copy; the original is in the British Museum.
31	The Erechtheum (west flank): on the left the north porch, the main entrance to the cella of Poseidon-Erechtheus. The Pandroseum stood on the empty space in the foreground. Here grew the mythical sacred olive tree of Athene; the one growing here today is, of course, younger. The tomb of Cecrops was in the background, where the metal column stands. On this plate the three porches of the Erechtheum can be seen. In the middle, the cella of Athena Polias. On the right the south porch, that of the Caryatids, and on the left the north porch.
32	The Erechtheum (north porch): magnificent Ionic columns with their ornamentation; in the background the main entrance to the cella of Poseidon-Erechtheus. The small door in the background, to the right, led to the Pandroseum. The ceiling coffers are worth noticing.
33	The Caryatids (back view).

THE ACROPOLIS MUSEUM

34	Museum No 35: a detail of plate 36 (cf. commentary, infra).
35	Mus. No 1, Room I: archaic pediment of tufa, which decorated a treasury of the 6th century B. C. The oldest surviving poros sculpture from the Acropolis. Coloured bas-relief depicting the fight of Heracles with the nine-headed Hydra of the Lernaean Spring. His friend Iolaus encourages him from his chariot. In the left-hand angle a huge crab sent by Hera to help the Hydra.
36	Mus. No 35, Room II: the two angles of an Archaic pediment of tufa. 570 B. C. On the left, Heracles locked in combat with Triton (a merman: half human, half fish), whose tail fills the left angle of the pediment. On the right, the monster with the three winged, human bodies which merge below the trunk into three-intertwined dragon tails of many colours. The identification of this monster with the three gay, bearded faces and the big laughing eyes is disputed (Typhon? Nereus? Geryon?). Each figure holds a symbol of one of the three " elements " in his hand: the one on the right a bird, the one in the middle surging water, the one on the left flames. According to W. B. Dinsmoor, these poros sculptures adorned the east pediment of the old Hecatompedon, i. e. the " original Parthenon " (cf. text, p. 15). The centre of this pediment was taken up by the large sculpture of the bull being killed by two lions (Mus. No 3).
37	Mus. No 701, Room I. Archaic Gorgon's head. Fragment of a central acroteria figure which stood on the apex of the pediment of an archaic temple. Early 6th cent. B. C.
38 39	Mus. No 55 + 9, Room II: the " Apotheosis of Heracles ". Small Archaic pediment in tufa (c. 580 B. C.). Heracles appears before the gods on Olympus. In the centre, Zeus (depicted in profile) seated on his throne, next to him Hera. Figure No 55 belongs to this same pediment.
40	Mus. No 52, Room II: small Archaic pediment of tufa (known as the " Olive-Tree Pediment ", 6th century B. C.). On this pediment, a Doric building is represented in high relief, perhaps the ancient Erechtheum with the sacred olive tree in the background. In front of the entrance a woman, perhaps the priestess of Athene, stands watching a retreating procession of men and women.

41	Mus. No 4, Room I: part of an Archaic pediment of tufa, a lioness devouring a young bull. The same theme was repeated opposite. According to Dinsmoor this central pedimental section comes from the west pediment of the Hecatompedon. In this case, the two fat serpentine monsters Nos 37 and 40 would belong in the angles of this pediment.
42	Mus. No 3, Room III: central section of an Archaic pediment in tufa (570—566 B. C.). A bull is being torn to pieces by two lions, of which, however, we only see the great paws (17 1/2 ft long). The colours are well preserved. This group formed the centre of the east pediment of the Hecatompedon; the two angles were filled by the sculptures of No 36 (cf. supra). The head of the bull is portrayed with great power.
43	Mus. No 575, Room II: four marble horses (seen from the front), which probably drew a chariot painted or shown in bas-relief, with the charioteer, on the wall behind. Archaic group from Attica (c. 570 B. C.).
44—46	Mus. No 624, Room II: the " Moschophoros " (Archaic statue in marble from Mt. Hymettus. Over 5 ft high). Attic sculpture of c. 570 B. C. The Moschophoros (" Calf-Bearer ") carries on his broad shoulders a young calf which he intends to offer to the goddess. The short garment he is wearing hugs his body. His cheerful face, framed by his hair which adorns his forehead like a cap of pearl's, and hangs down over his shoulders, his eyes wide open — originally inlaid with stones — his smiling mouth and well-shaped beard, all these are signs of the Archaic character of this interesting statue. A half-obliterated inscription on the base gives the name of the donor as (Rh)ombos or (K)ombos.
47	Mus. No 630, Room II: Archaic sphinx of Pentelic marble, 560 B. C. Burn marks. Height: 2 ft. One of the oldest statues which witnesses to the Ionian influence on Attic sculpture.
48	Mus. No 593, Room II: The Kore with the Pomegranate, the oldest of the Archaic kores (c. 570 B. C.). In marble. Height: over 3 ft. Found in 1887 east of the Erechtheum. The kore's head is missing. She is wearing a chiton with sleeves and over this a Dorian peplus and an himation which hangs symmetrically over the shoulders and covers her back. In her right hand, she holds a wreath, and in her left hand, in front of her breast, a pomegranate.
49	Mus. No 581, Athena, detail of a votive relief representing a family carrying offerings to Athena. (c. 500 B. C.)
50	Mus. No 677, Room III: the Naxian Kore. A bust, part of a marble statue from the island of Naxos. 1 3/4 ft high. First half of the 6th century. The kore is wearing a beautifully draped Ionian chiton and is offering an apple in her left hand, which is held in front of her breast.
51 52	Mus. No 590, Room IV: the Rampin Rider. An equestrian statue of Parian marble. The head, which has been in the Louvre since 1875, measures 11 1/2 inches in height. The body, which was found 11 years later on the Acropolis (in 1886 west of the Erechtheum) is 2 2/3 ft in height. The head shown here is a plaster cast. The two parts of the Rider were first linked by the English archaeologist Payne. This is the oldest Greek equestrian statue. The rider sits upright on his horse, with his head turned somewhat to the left and wearing a friendly smile on his face. His hair appears severely stylised. Loving treatment of details is coupled with Archaic severity. The Rider wears a garland of ivy on his head which leads us to suppose that he won the garland as a prize at the Nemean Games. 560 B. C.
53	Mus. No 136. Fragment of a statue. Parian marble. " The foot is unsurpassed in all archaic sculpture and from it one may safely infer that the statue was a masterpiece." H. Payne, 495 B. C.
54	Mus. No 69: sima (corner stone), a spout from the guttering of the temple of Athena Polias. A lion's head in island marble. Height: 10 1/2 in. 520 B. C. Probably a magnificent late production of the master of No. 590.
55	Mus. No 143: hunting-dog, tensed to spring on its prey. Island marble. Lenght: little over 4 ft, height: 1 3/4 ft. The vivid and powerful treatment of the subject points to an artist of great ability. Probably a votive offering for the temenos of Artemis Brauronia, the patroness of the hunt, 520 B. C.
56	Mus. No 606: the Persian Rider. Fragment of a rider (c. 520 B. C.). Island

marble. 3 1/4 ft high. The red boots and the colourful oriental costume are characteristic of Scythian or Persian dress. Probably an ex voto of an Attic nobleman who, like Miltiades, had property in " barbarian " territory.

57 Mus. No 700: horse and the feet of its rider (c. 500 B. C.). Pentelic marble. Height 3 2/3 ft; length: 2 1/2 ft. The elegant and proud posture of this Archaic horse calls to mind the splendour-loving times of the Pisistratidae, with the horse races and the cavalcade of the Panathenaic procession. These equestrian sculptures reached their perfection in the Parthenon frieze by Phidias.

58 59 120 Mus. No 679: kore with Dorian peplus, Parian marble (c. 530 B. C.). Total height: 4 ft. Found 1886 west of the Erechtheum. This Peplus Kore is one of the most beautiful. Whereas all her companions dating from roughly the same period have all adopted the new Ionian fashion, she still wears with pride and a smile of cheerful composure, the simple, almost-entirely-undraped Dorian peplus. Beneath the hem of the peplus the finely pleated chiton is to be seen. In spite of an element of Archaic severity in the overall composition, the sculptor, certainly one of the great masters of his time (perhaps the creator of Nos 590, 69 and 143), has been able to animate and — especially by the expression of the face and above all in the eyes — enliven the Peplus Kore by his loving attention to detail. The colouring is in part well preserved. About kores in general, cf. text, pp. 17, 18).

60 62 Mus. No 673: Archaic kore of Pentelic marble (c. 520 B. C.). Attic. A peculiarity in her dress: the himation is fastened at both shoulders, so that it descends on both sides in perpendicular folds. On the kore's head we see the " meniskos ". an iron spike, still nearly 5 in. long, intended to stop larger birds settling on the statue.

61 63 Mus. No 675: Archaic kore of marble from the island of Chios (510 B. C.). Height (head and torso): 1 3/4 ft. The head was found in 1886 to the east, the torso in 1888 to the south of the Parthenon. Small Ionian kore from Chios. The gay colours of its clothing are well preserved, probably because it stood indoors. This also explains why it has no meniskos. The upper part of the chiton still has its beautiful blue-green colour. The himation, too, with its wide border round the neck and upper arm, still has the deep blue and the red of the embroidery. The hair falls in curls over the forehead. The gentle lines of the face offer a typical example of the " Archaic smile ".

64—67 Mus. No 682: large Archaic kore of island marble (c. 525 B. C.). Burn marks. Found in 1886, north-west of the Erechtheum. Total height: 6 ft. The most characteristic and best preserved of the Ionian kores on the Acropolis. Her posture is proud; an " Archaic smile ", which appears slightly ironical, plays across the decisive lines of her face with its slanting eyes. Her luxurious hairstyle employs four different types of tresses. The costume she wears is costly and of studied elegance. The colours are well preserved. The sculptor shows his gifts in his attention to detail. Meniskos.

68—70 Mus. No 684: Archaic kore of island marble, c. 490 B. C. Found 1882/83, east of the Parthenon. Height: 4 ft. The artist, who produced this kore obviously attached less importance to decorative elements; the kore conveys a more serious and natural impression and is thus more effective than the others.

71—74 123 Mus. No 674: Archaic kore of Parian marble. Height: 3 ft. Attic, c. 500 B. C. One of the most beautiful of the kores in the museum, of delicate female grace and maidenly reserve, in many details a counterpiece to the extrovert kore No 682. The hair is arranged in waves which cover the temples; the eyes are black; the face has a delicate yellow patina. The slim neck appears to be especially accentuated by the gentle slope of the shoulders. The chiton still bears its beautiful colours. (Plate 123) This statue was found south-west of the Parthenon in 1886.

Cover Photo and 75—78 Mus. No 670: Archaic kore of island marble (520 B. C.). 3 3/4 ft high. This kore was found north-west of the Erechtheum in 1886. Attic work. Extremely graceful and attractive, like a little princess. She is wearing only a finely pleated (or knitted) chiton, caught in at the waist so that a kind of billowing fold descends to her hips (kolpos). With her left hand she gently raises this garment in front which accordingly falls in elegant folds. Probably from the same hand as kore No. 673.

79	Mus. No 643: head of an Archaic kore of Parian marble (c. 510 B. C.). Yellow patina. 5 ½ in. high. One of the masterpieces of Attic sculpture.
80	Mus. No 625: seated Athene, torso, of island marble. Height: nearly 5 ft. According to Pausanias, who saw this statue, dedicated by a certain Callias, on the Acropolis in the 2nd century A. D., it was a work of the sculptor Endoeus. Athene's aegis, with the Gorgoneion at the centre, covers her breast and back. The tensing of the body suggests that Athene is just about to rise. Found in 1821, on the northern slope of the Erechtheum.
81 82	Mus. No 633: Young man in ankle-lenght garment (c. 510). Parian marble. 4 ft high. Shows great similarity to kores of the same period. Only the hairstyle appears decidedly manly. The Ionian style laid greater emphasis on the general features of youth.
83—85	Mus. No 685: Archaic kore of island marble (500—490 B. C.). 4 ft high. Attic work. This kore is not wearing the Ionian smile, but a look of solemn gravity. She does not gather up her robe with the left hand like the other kores, but brings offerings in both hands, so that her finely draped, form-hugging chiton accentuates her slim form (cf. back view, Plate 83). Found south-west of the Parthenon in 1888.
86	Mus. No 680: Archaic kore, with an apple in her hand (530 B. C.). Island marble. 3 ¾ ft high. Burn marks. The embroidery of the borders of the himation and chiton is interesting and well preserved. Found north-west of the Erechtheum in 1886.
87 119	Mus. No 686: the "Kore of Euthydicus", so named after the donor (c. 485 B. C.). White marble. Burn marks. Hight: almost 2 ft. Found east of the Parthenon in 1882. The youngest of the Archaic kores, a purely Attic creation. This kore is Archaic only in dress and posture, otherwise conveys more the spirit of the pre-Classical period. The waves of the hair are parted in the middle. The face is very regular and harmonious. The line of the eyes is horizontal. The nickname, "the Pouting Maiden", does not really do justice to the recollected seriousness of the noble face.
88	Mus. No 671: large Archaic kore of Pentelic marble (520 B. C.). 5 ¾ ft high. Chiton like that of kore No 670. Over it she is wearing a cloak, the himation. A slight smile plays over the features of her face. Found west of the Erechtheum in 1886.
89 90	Mus. No 683, A strange little kore. She wears red shoes and holds a bird in her left hand. (c. 510 B. C.).
91	Marble head of a snake which decorated the aegis of Athena.
92	A small bronze boar.
93	Mus. No 681: the "Kore of Antenor". Large kore of island marble. Height: 6 ½ ft. This is the only one among all the kores which has the name of its artist on the base, although it is not absolutely certain that the base bearing the name of the sculptor Antenor belongs to this statue, alongside of which it was found. Antenor, one of the great sculptors of his day, produced the plastic decoration for the east pediment of the temple of Apollo which the Alcmaeonidae commissioned at Delphi. He was also the artist of the Tyrannicides which Xerxes carried off to Persia. The name "Nearchus" can also be read on the base of the statue; this is presumably the name of the donor. The strong emphasis placed on the perpendicular makes this kore appear decidedly monumental in character. The face is damaged. A diadem, surmounted by a meniskos, crowns the kore's forehead.
94	Mus. No 698: the "Critius Boy", of Parian marble and 2 ¾ ft high. The body was found south-east of the Parthenon in 1866, the head in 1888. The statue of a naked and standing youth. The hair is wound round the head like a garland. Characteristic is the treatment of the boy's body, which betrays the transition from the Archaic to the Classical style. The left leg bears the weight of the body; the body is turned slightly on its axis. This work was produced shortly before the battle of Salamis (480 B. C.) and is ascribed to the famous sculptor Critius.
95	Mus. No 695: the "Sorrowing Athene" or "Athene with the Lance (460 B. C.). Votive relief in Parian marble. Height 1 ¾ ft. Found south of the Parthenon. This is one of the best Attic reliefs in the "severe style": Athene,

with helmet and a simple Attic Peplus (without aegis or Gorgoneion), leans her head pensively against her lance and seems to be studying the inscription on the stele (funerary stele?).

96 Mus. No 1332: the Potter (510 B. C.). Relief in Pentelic marble. Height: 4 ft, width: 2 1/2 ft. Votive relief depicting a potter sitting in a diphros (armchair). The arrangement of the hair and beard is Archaic.

97 98 Mus. No 689: the "Blond Boy" (c. 480 B. C.). Head in Pentelic marble. 10 in. high. A fragment of the body was also found. The head is almost undamaged. The hair falls down in waves over both forehead and temples, where it covers the two tresses, which, crossed at the nape of the neck, encircle the head like a wreath. The statue is so named because of the traces of yellow paint to be seen in the hair. The somewhat dreamy expression of the eyes and the serious look on the face impart an air of melancholy to the "Blond Boy", who could well be the younger brother of the "Kore of Euthydicus". Both are works of a great but anonymous sculptor.

99 100 Two plaster-cast attempted reconstructions of the Parthenon pediments. These reconstructions are based on the drawings of Jacques Carrey or of an unknown painter who accompanied the Marquis de Nointel when he visited the Acropolis in 1674 (hence before the great catastrophe caused by Morosini in 1687). At this time the pediments were still almost intact. The arrangement and identification of the figures is disputed.

101 Mus. No 697: horse in the "severe style". Island marble. Height: 3 3/4 ft, length: 1 1/2 ft. The winnying of this proud horse heralds the splendid cavalcade of the Panathenaic Procession. 490—480 B. C.

102 Mus. No 885: Torso of Poseidon. From the west pediment of the Parthenon. From the studio of Phidias, 440—432 B. C. Pentelic marble. (Cf. text, p. 27). Unfortunately only a part of the trunk is original, the remainder is a plaster cast of the fragment preserved in the British Museum.

103—110 Panathenaic Procession. Sculptures from the Parthenon frieze. In Pentelic marble. Height: 3 1/3 ft. (cf. text, p. 19).

103 104 Mus. No 857, north frieze. Three young men are leading their oxen to be sacrificed. Detail of the head of the leading youth.

105 Mus. No 865: north frieze. The "Thallophoroi", venerable old men, holding olive branches and following the procession.

106 Mus. No 864: north frieze. The Olympian gods: Poseidon, Apollo and Artemis, who are watching the Panathenaic procession and the bringing of the peplus.

108 Mus. No 863: north frieze. The cavalcade. The man in the centre, back to back with one of the riders, is an official directing the procession. A composition masterly in its compactness. In the Acropolis museum there are on view 20 original panels from the frieze: 13 from the north, 5 from the south and 2 from the east wall.

109 Mus. No 860: north frieze. A shepherd leading his sheep to be sacrificed.

110 Mus. No 862: north frieze. Detail, head of a rider.

111 112 Two winged Nikes (410—409 B. C.). Reliefs from the parapet which encircled the pyrgos of the temple of Athene Nike. Executed in Pentelic marble. Height: 3 1/2 ft. (Cf. text, p. 29).

111 Mus. No 972: a winged Nike leads an unruly bull to the sacrifice. The head-on wind seems to spur the Nike on. Remarkable here is the impression of dynamic movement which the composition conveys.

112 Mus. No 973: one of the most beautiful reliefs in the museum. A winged Nike is just loosening one of her sandals in order to approach the altar of sacrifice barefooted. Although only a torso, the work moves us by the youthful grace of the figure and the wonderful drapery of the attractive garment. It is the work of some great but unknown master.

113 Mus. No 1338: votive bas-relief on a marble socle, dated 322 B. C., depicts the dancers taking part in the "Phyrric", a war dance, during which the dancers mimed all the phases and movements of assault and defence. According to the legend, Athene was the first to perform this dance; she then taught it to men.

114   Mus. No 989: a relief from the south-western corner of the same parapet of the temple of Athena Nike. Athene sits on a throne of rocks and rests her right arm on her shield. In front, a winged Nike hands the goddess one of her victory trophies.

115   Mus. No 1339: Bas-relief in marble, found on the Acropolis in 1852, depicts an Attic " trireme " (c. 400 B. C.). Probably part of a victory monument, dedicated to Athene after the successful outcome of a battle at sea. Triremes were warships with three banks of oars on both sides.

116   Mus. No 1345—6464. Two pieces of reliefs representing three Nymphs and the goat's feet of Pan sitting on a rock. 2nd—Ist cent. B. C.

117   Mus. No 1326. Votive bas-relief on a marble socle, (3rd century B. C.) depicts a four-horse chariot with his charioteer and an " apobate ". The " apobate " was jumping off and on the chariot during the race.

118   Mus. No 1358. Statue of Prokne with her son Itys, whom she intends to kill, like the legendary Medea. The sculptor of this statue was perhaps Alkamenes, a pupil of Phidias. (c. 420 B. C.)

119   Mus. No 686: The " Euthydikos Kore ", cf. No 87

120   Mus. No 679: The Peplus Kore, cf. No 58

121   Mus. No 1331: portrait in marble of Alexander the Great (c. 335 B. C.). Perhaps a work of Leochares who executed portraits of Alexander several times while he and Lysippus resided at Alexander's court as sculptors.

122   Mus. No 1313: portrait of a Neo-Platonic Philosopher (c. 430 A. D.).

123   Mus. No 674: Archaic Kore of Parian marble (cf. No 73)

The Acropolis seen from the Temple of Olympian Zeus
◁   1   L'Acropole vue du haut du Temple de Zeus Olympien
Die Akropolis, vom Olympion (Ruinen des Zeustempels) aus

The Acropolis seen from Philopappos' hill
2   L'Acropole vue de la colline Mouseion ou Philopappos
Die Akropolis vom Philopappos-Hügel aus

The Acropolis seen from the Piraeus
3 L'Acropole vue du Pirée
Blick über den Hafen Piräus auf die Akropolis

The Acropolis seen from the Areopagus
4   L'Acropole vue de l'Aréopage
Die Akropolis vom Areopag aus

The Acropolis, illuminated
5   L'Acropole illuminée
Die Akropolis, illuminiert

The Acropolis from the west
6　L'Acropole vue de l'ouest
Die Akropolis von Westen

7

General view from the Acropolis towards the sea

Vue générale du haut de l'Acropole vers la mer et le golfe Saronique

Blick von der Akropolis zum Saronischen Golf und Aegäischen Meer (Inseln Salamis, rechts, Ägina, links und Peloponnes-Gebirge)

ΛΙΣ

Temple of Athena Nike
9   Temple d' Athéna Niké
Tempel der Athena Nike

The Propylaea
10 Les Propylées
Die Propyläen

Ionic column in the Propylaea
13 Colonne ionique des Propylées
Ionische Säule der Propyläen

Remains of the Propylaea
of Pisistratus
14 Restes des Propylées de Pisistrate ▷
Reste der früheren Propyläen
des Pisistratus

The Parthenon from the Propylaea
15 16 Le Parthénon vu des Propylées
Der Parthenon, von den Propyläen aus

Interior of the Parthenon
17 18 Intérieur du Parthénon
Inneres des Parthenon

The Parthenon from north-east
19 Le Parthénon vu du nord-est
Der Parthenon von Nord-Ost

Details of the east pediment of the Parthenon
20 Détails du fronton est du Parthénon
Details der Ostfront des Parthenon

21
The Parthenon from north-west
Le Parthénon vu du nord-ouest
Der Parthenon von Nord-West

Details from the west frieze of the Parthenon
22 23 24   Détails de la frise ouest du Parthénon
Details des Westfrieses des Parthenon

South colonnade of the Parthenon
29 Colonnade sud du Parthénon   ▷
Süd-Kolonnade des Parthenon

Inside of the Parthenon (after a rain)
28 Intérieur du Parthénon (après la pluie)
Inneres des Parthenon (nach Regen)

The Caryatides
30 Le Portique des Caryatides
Die Korenhalle, Karyatiden

Erechtheion, north portico
32 Erechthéion, portique du nord   ▷
Nördliche Säulenhalle des Erechtheion

Erechtheion from the west
31 L'Erechthéion vu de l'ouest
Erechtheion von Westen

34   Museum No. 35, Detail

ACROPOLIS MUSEUM
MUSÉE DE L' ACROPOLE
AKROPOLISMUSEUM

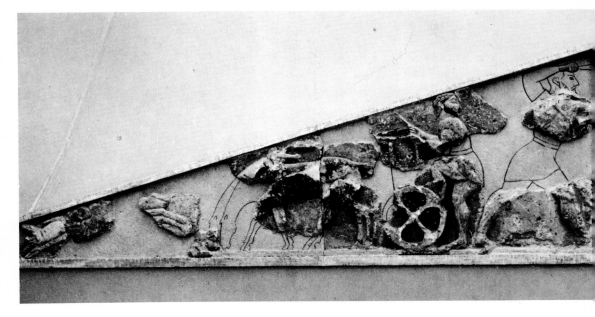

35 Mus. No. 1   Pediment of Heracles and the Hydra

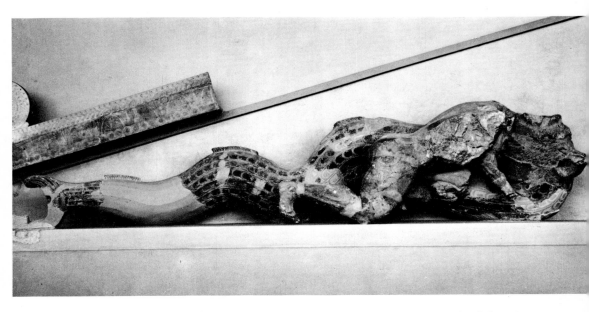

36 Mus. No. 35   Archaic pediment of the three-headed monster

Fronton d'Héraclès tuant l'Hydra   Tuffgiebel: Herakles tötet die Hydra

Fronton archaïque du monstre aux trois corps   Archaischer Giebel mit dem Drei-Körper-Monstrum

37   Mus. No. 701
Archaic gorgon's head
Tête archaïque du Méduse
Medusenhaupt, archaisch

55

38 39   Mus. No. 55   9
"The apotheosis of Heracles." An archaic limestone pediment
« L'apothéose d'Héraclès. » Fronton archaïque en pôros
Die Apotheose des Herakles. Archaischer Tuffsteingiebel

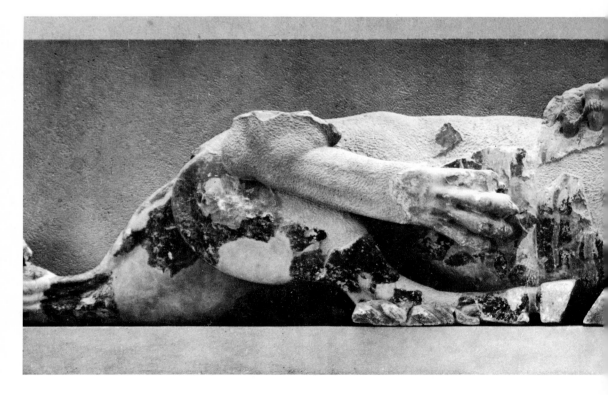

40 41 42 Mus. No. 52 4 3
Three different archaic limestone pediments
Trois fontons archaïques en pôros différents
Drei archaische Tuffsteingiebel

Reconstructio ad Mus. No. 3

43 Mus. No. 575
An Early Attic group. Four frontal horses with chariot
Char à quatre chevaux vu de front. Groupe archaïque de l'Attique
Frontales Vierpferdegespann. Archaisches Werk aus Attika

44 Mus. No. 624
The Moschophoros, a man carrying a calf
Le Moschophore
Der Moschophoros (Opfertierträger)

45 46 Mus. No. 624
The Moschophoros, a man carrying a calf
Le Moschophore
Der Moschophoros (Opfertierträger)

48   Mus. No. 593
The earliest of the Korai holding a pomegranate
La Coré à la grenade, la plus ancienne des corés
Kore mit Granatapfel, die früheste der Korenfiguren

47   Mus. No. 630
An early Attic Sphinx
Sphinx archaïque
Archaische Sphinx

51 52 Mus. No. 590
The Rampin horseman
Le Cavalier Rampin
Der Rampin-Reiter

54   Mus. No. 69
A spout from the sima of the Temple of Athena Polias
Gouttière de la corniche du temple d'Athéna Polias
Wasserspeier vom Dach des Tempels der Athena Polias

55   Mus. No. 143
A dog, offering in the precinct of Artemis Brauronia
Chien de chasse, offrande dans le Sanctuaire d'Artémis Brauronia
Jagdhund, Opfer aus dem Heiligtum der Artemis Brauronia

53   Mus. No. 136
Fragment of a statue. The foot is a masterpiece of archaic sculpture
Fragment d'une statue. Le pied est un chef-d'œuvre de la sculpture archaïque
Bruchstück einer Statue. Der Fuß ist ein Meisterstück der archaischen Skulptur

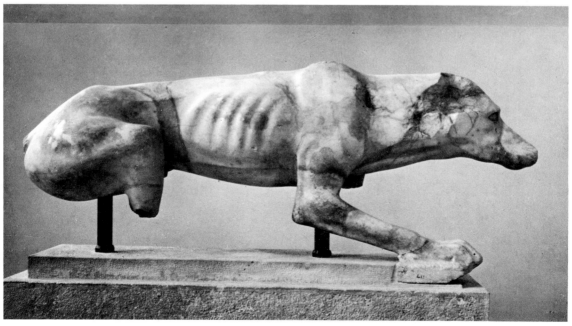

56 Mus. No. 606
Fragment of a horseman and horse
Fragment d'un cavalier à cheval
Bruchstück eines Reiters mit Pferd

57 Mus. No. 700
Horse and part of the horseman
Cheval et fragment de son cavalier
Pferd und Fragment des Reiters

64 Mus. No. 682

65   Mus. No. 682

66   Mus. No. 682

67   Mus. No. 682

68 Mus. No. 684

69 Mus. No. 684

71 Mus. No. 674

73 Mus. No. 674

74   Mus. No. 674

75   Mus. No. 670

76   Mus. No. 670

77   Mus. No. 670

78   Mus. No. 670

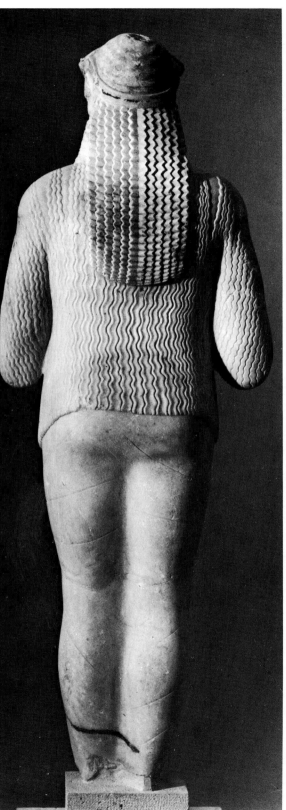

80 Mus. No. 625 Athena, by Endoios   Athéna, œuvre d'Endoios   Athena, Werk des Endoios

81 82 Mus. No. 633 Draped youth Jeune homme drapé Bekleideter Jüngling

◁
87   Mus. No. 686
The ' Euthidikos Kore '
« La Coré d'Euthidikos »
,,Die Euthidikos-Kore"

88   Mus. No. 671   ▷

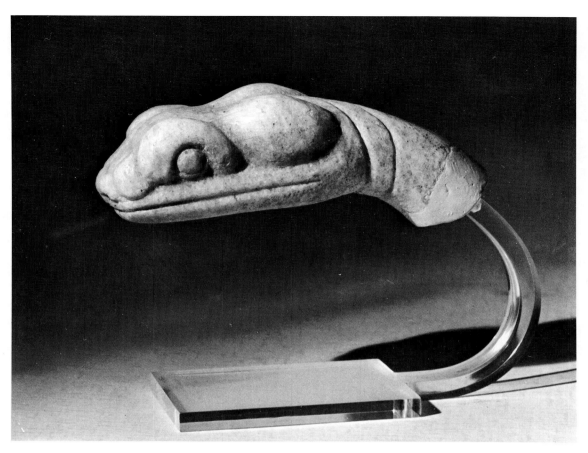

Marble head of a snake
91 Tête de serpent en marbre
Kopf einer Schlange, Marmor

Small bronze boar
92 Petit sanglier en bronze
Wildschwein, kleine Bronzefigur

93   Mus. No. 681
"Antenor's Kore"
« La Coré d'Anténor »
,,Die Kore des Antenor"

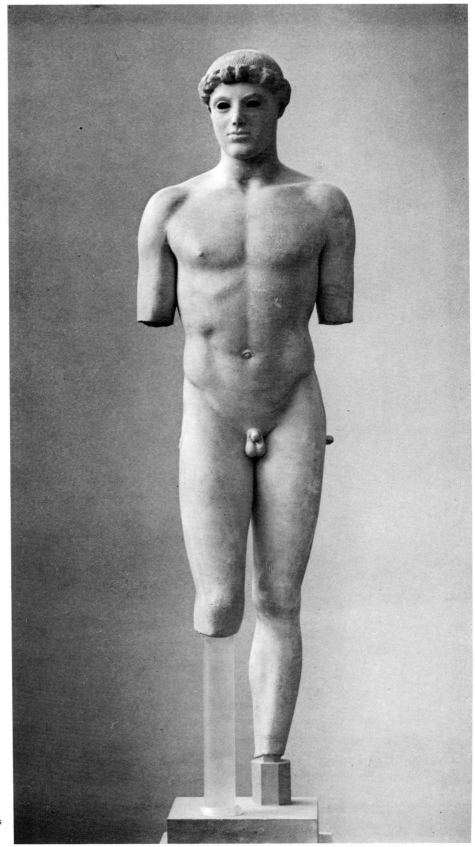

94 Mus. No. 698
The 'Kritian boy'
L'Ephèbe de Critios
Der Kritiosknabe

95 Mus. No. 695
The 'Mourning Athene'
« L'Athéna mélancolique »
„Die Trauernde Athene"

96 Mus. No. 1332
The potter
Le potier
Der Töpfer ▷

97 98 Mus. No. 689   The 'Blond boy'

« L'Ephèbe blond »   „Der blonde Jüngling"

Helios   Dionysos   Demeter   Persephone   Eileithyia   Ares   Eros   Aphrodite   Hera   Zeus

Kephissos   Eridanos   Kekrops   Pandrosos   Aglauros   Erychthonios   Herse   Nike   Hermes   Athena

99 100
Reconstruction of Parthenon's pediment sculptures
Reconstitution des sculptures des frontons du Parthénon
Rekonstruktion der Giebel-Skulpturen des Parthenon

Athena   Hephaistos   Poseidon   Apollon   Artemis   Hermes   Clotho   Lachesis   Atropos   Selene

East pediment   Fronton est   Ostgiebel

Iris   Amphitrite   Oreithya   Ion   Kreusa   Prokris   Ilissos   Kallirrhoe

West pediment   Fronton ouest   Westgiebel

102   Mus. No. 885
Torso of Poseidon by Phidias from the west pediment of the Parthenon
Buste de Poseidon par Phidias. Fronton ouest du Parthénon
Torso des Poseidon von Phidias aus dem westlichen Giebel des Parthenon

◁ 101 Mus. No. 697   Horse   Cheval   Roß

103 104 Mus. No. 857
Sculptures from the Parthenon. Relief from the north frieze: The Panathenaic procession and detail
Sculptures du Parthénon. Frise Nord. La Procession des Panathénées et détail
Skulpturen des Parthenon. Nordfries. Panathenäischer Festzug und Detail

105 106   Mus. No. 865 864
Sculptures from the Parthenon. Reliefs from the north frieze: The Panathenaic procession
Sculptures du Parthénon. Frise Nord. La Procession des Panathénées
Skulpturen des Parthenon. Nordfries. Panathenäischer Festzug

107 Mus. No. 856
From the east frieze of the Parthenon: Poseidon, Apollo and Artemis
Frise est du Parthénon: Poseidon, Apollon et Artémis
Ostfries des Parthenon: Poseidon, Apollon und Artemis

109 110   Mus. No. 860 862
Sculptures from the Parthenon. North frieze: The Panathenaic procession (details)
Sculptures du Parthénon. Frise Nord. La Procession des Panathénées (détails)   ▷
Skulpturen des Parthenon. Nordfries. Panathenäischer Festzug (Details)

111 112   Mus. No. 972 973
Two winged Nikes from the balustrade round the Temple of Athena Nike
Deux Nikés ailées, relief de la balustrade qui entourait le Temple d'Athéna Niké   ▷ ▷
Zwei geflügelte Niken von der Brüstung des Athena-Nike-Tempels

108   Mus. No. 863
Equestrian relief from the north frieze of the Parthenon
Procession des cavaliers de la frise Nord du Parthénon
Reiterfestzug vom Nordfries des Parthenon

113   Mus. No. 1338   Votive relief representing a Pyrrhic Dance (war-dance)

114   Mus. No. 989

Athena and a winged
Nike

Athéna et une Niké
ailée

Athena und eine geflü-
gelte Nike

Bas-relief votif représentant une dance Pyrrhique   Votivrelief: Pyrrhischer Tanz (Kriegertanz)

15   Mus. No. 1339

Marble Bas-relief of
n Athenian Trireme
warship)

Bas-relief en marbre
'une trière
thénienne

Marmorrelief   einer
thenischen   Triere
Kriegsschiff)

116   Mus. No. 1345 6464
The nymphs reliefs
Reliefs des nymphes
Nymphenreliefs

117   Mus. No. 1326
Marble votive relief
Bas-relief votif en marbre
Votivrelief aus Marmor

118   Mus. No. 1358
Procne and Itys
Procné avec Itys
Prokne mit Itys

△ 120　Mus. No. 679　　The Peplos Kore　　La Coré au péplos　　Die Peplos-Kore

◁ 119　Mus. No. 686　　The 'Euthydikos Kore'　　« La Coré d'Euthydicos »　　„Die Euthydikos-Kore"

121 Mus. No. 1331
Portrait of Alexander the Great
◁ Portrait d'Alexandre le Grand
Portätkopf: Alexander der Große

122 Mus. No. 1313
Portrait of a Neoplatonist Philosopher
Portrait d'un philosophe néo-platonicien
Porträt eines Neuplatonischen Philosophen